AMISH
CANNING & PRESERVING
COOKBOOK

HOW TO MAKE CHUTNEYS, JAMS, JELLIES, SAUCES, COUP AND MORE

BY
SHIRLEY BISHOP

TABLE OF CONTENTS

Chapter 5: Main Foods   72

Chapter 6: Fruits and Vegetables 124

Chapter 7: Jelly and Syrup — 156

Chapter 8: Chutney and Marmalade   174

Chapter 9: Pickles and Relish   196

Chapter 10: Salsa and Sauces   220

TABLE OF CONTENTS

INTRODUCTION

Canning is one of the oldest methods of food preservation.

Canning allows you to store a variety of meals such as meats, vegetables, soups, fruits, sauces, and so on.

Home canning has become a popular option for many people who want to avoid the high prices of store-canned foods. However, it will necessitate a thorough understanding of the processes involved. This book will teach you everything you need to know about Amish canning and include 200 healthy, delicious recipes that you can make at home.

Canning is a method of preserving food by placing it in jars or cans and heating it to a specific temperature.

This book provides tried-and-true Amish canning methods for your kitchen. Preserving is an alchemical art, and experimentation with food is encouraged. While there are some rules to follow, there is also plenty of room for creativity. With that in mind, the central underlying theme of this book is food alters life, and life alters food, and preserving allows us to remember and celebrate this on a daily basis.

If you use a current canning recipe and keep your kitchen clean, everything will turn out perfectly. Canning is an important and safe technique for food preservation when done correctly.

Food preservation is a technique that has been used for centuries. It has been a preservation technique that has assisted humans in surviving harsh weather and climate. Preservation techniques have improved over time. There are, however, some basic preservation techniques that you can use at home to easily preserve foods.

Canning is a time-tested method of storing food, such as fruits, for an extended period. If you use the canning technique regularly, it will be very beneficial to you. However, some rules and instructions must be followed for the technique to be successful.

Whether you're new to canning or have been storing food for years,

The Amish Canning Cookbook will find a home in your kitchen. You can also be certain that the information in these recipes is up to date. The recipes on this page aren't fancy, but they are family-friendly. This is terrific, nourishing food that can serve as the foundation for many great dinners, and even the pickiest eaters will appreciate the results of your efforts.

Let's get started!

CHAPTER 1
WHAT IS CANNING AND PRESERVING

Canning is a practice born out of necessity when people did not have access to electricity or a fridge. It allowed them to preserve their food for much longer, which could help them when there was less food to go around. Nowadays, it is more of a fun practice as you already have access to a fridge. But this activity is synonymous with those who own a garden in the backyard, and maybe that is you. You planted your seeds, tended to them, and took care of them all summer. Eventually, you harvested the fruit of your labor (literally), and they ended up on your dinner plate.

Job well done, you thought. Except, there was a tiny problem. You got too much food on your hands. You can only enjoy your homegrown cucumber for so long before you turn it into a cucumber, but leaving them out would not be healthy for the harvest as well, so what can you do? This is where canning comes in, a very effective way to store your fruits and veggies while they are in season. Done properly, you can keep them relatively fresh, long enough until the next season comes around. Pretty convenient!

Canning is a simple, inexpensive, effective, and safe method of preserving food without the use of chemicals or other additives. This simple method can be used to shelf-stable fresh fruits and vegetables, cooked sauces, and many different types of meals in a jar. The procedure is actually quite straightforward. To stop the bacterial growth and oxidation process, the food is placed in a nonreactive jar or can with a liquid, and the jar is placed and boiled in a water bath or pressure bath. When the food is highly acidic and has the lowest pH value, microorganisms can be destroyed at normal boiling temperatures. When the food is significantly less acidic, however, extremely high boiling temperatures are required to kill the microorganisms. This is why canning works better for preserving food than boiling or cooking. The pH and temperature of the food are both optimized during canning to prevent spoilage due to bacterial or fungal growth. In this manner, the food is preserved for a longer time.

Canning is a food preservation technique that involves sealing foods in airtight containers and boiling them for a set amount of time. Because refrigeration was not widely available until recently, it was the only way to store leftovers from summer picnics or holiday feasts. Most commercially canned foods are heated in a water bath inside the container, which means they are not sealed inside an airtight container before being processed under pressure with steam.

Pressure canners operate in a unique manner, sealing foods in airtight containers with the lid locked in place before placing them inside a sealed vessel.

The air pressure around the food is raised to at least 10 lb per square inch (psi), which kills any microorganisms that could cause foodborne illness. Each food requires a different level of processing pressure.

Canning jars are made of tempered glass and come in a variety of sizes, the most common being 6- or 8-ounce jars. The standard canner has a capacity of seven-quart jars or nine-pint jars. Never fill a jar more than halfway because it needs room to expand when boiling. The lids can be reused if they are not bent or rusted. In any case, they should be replaced after one use for any food that isn't commercially canned.

The most important thing to remember about canning is that no steps, especially those related to food safety, should be skipped. That's why every jar of canned food has a "use by" or "sell by" date to remind consumers that the food is safe to eat, even after it's been processed. Because perishable foods degrade quickly at room temperature, the "sell by" date also informs stores when to remove the product from their shelves. The "use by" date indicates whether the canned goods are still safe to consume after the expiration date.

Canning is a great way to keep fruits and vegetables from the garden or farmer's market fresh while they're still in season. It extends the bounty into the winter when locally and seasonally available items are scarce. Canning extends the shelf life of products significantly, and food remains edible for much longer than it would otherwise. According to studies, canned foods have the same nutritional value as fresh foods and can even serve as healthier alternatives.

Canning is a process of preserving food in jars at high temperatures for an extended length of time, killing microorganisms and neutralizing enzymes that would otherwise cause food to spoil. As the food cools, the heating process pushes air out of the jar, establishing a vacuum seal.

Benefits of Canning Your Food

Home canning is becoming increasingly important as food scarcity becomes a global issue and the population fights inflation in many economies. Going back to our roots and practicing home canning does not make us primitive; instead, it allows us to combine modern technology with primitive wisdom to increase food sustainability.

As food prices rise, home canning allows you to use different foods whenever you want and with zero waste. Furthermore, home canning is a fulfilling and rewarding process that you can reap the benefits of for months or years. Canning and preserving foods also allow you to enjoy local foods for an extended period of time.

You can easily package your favorite seasonal fruits and vegetables for later consumption. With home canning, you can enjoy an abundance of jellies, jams, and pickles whenever you want.

Home canning can be started as a hobby and a personal project. Following that, you can expand your preserving and home canning into a larger operation for your neighbors and community. Home-based canned product brands are emerging as people's demand for home-based brands and foods grows. You can even turn your home canning project into a profitable business with a large customer base. Who doesn't want healthy and delicious jams and marmalades?

Home canning extends the life of food and the jars in which it is stored. When you do home canning, you keep your batches in reusable glass jars rather than the disposable cans found at the supermarket. This reduces household waste and improves the green footprint of your domestic sphere. As a result, home canning is a process that every household should begin at some point. Home canning can also involve different family members and increase cooperation among family members.

Home canning is a process that has been prevalent for centuries, and some basic processes have not changed. If you connect with the roots of our foods, home canning is a hobby you should adopt.

Excellent Taste
The flavors of homemade dishes are preserved when they are canned. Canning at home allows you to maintain the authenticity of the ingredients while not sacrificing flavor.

Healthy
Food preserved through home canning contains no additives, making it healthier than store-bought items. They contain no chemicals because they are canned using only food and water canning or pressure equipment.

Preserve Seasonal Food
There are various seasonal fruits and vegetables. Canning such foods aid in long-term storage. If you buy those seasonal foods in excess, you can store the surplus at home using the canning procedure.

Environment Friendly
Canning is environmentally friendly because it requires no artificial preservation methods and saves a lot of food from spoiling and wasting. Unlike factory processing and canning, home canning allows you to reuse the same equipment without releasing any waste products.

Provides Food Security

When you don't have enough money to spend on food, canning can help you save for difficult days. If you are concerned about economic instability, you can always stockpile additional food by preserving it in large quantities. Canning allows for the safe storage of a wide range of foods while causing the least amount of harm and providing the greatest health advantages.

Saves Cost

Canning is a simple way of preserving food that does not require any chemicals or extra ingredients. It involves minimal equipment that you may reuse to can as much food as you like. Canning at home also reduces your reliance on store-bought canned or processed foods, which is beneficial for your wallet. By preserving food in this manner, you can also avoid wasting a lot of materials, which helps you save money.

Canning and Preserving Safety Tips

There are many safety tips that the canning process needs to progress through. Every process has some safety precautions that the person has to follow. Only with these canning and preservation safety tips will you be able to recreate canning recipes properly.

Select the Best Canner

The basic tip you should follow for safety and successful completion of the process is to select the right canner. There are various types of canners for various types of canned foods. Make sure that you choose a pressure canner or a water bath canner based on your needs and recipes. The canner must be new or well-maintained for there to be no problems during the canning process. The canner is an important part of the processing steps for home-canned recipes, and you must select the right one.

Select a Screw-Top Lid System

When selecting jars and lids for home canning vessels, make sure the jars have a screw-top lid system so that the lids can be tightly sealed during canning. The metal screw band is essential during the sealing process, but it should be removed once the canning process is complete. You can reuse the screw bands, but you must discard any rusted or damaged screw bands after each canning process. For tightening and sealing the jar mouth, the screw lid system is ideal.

Examine Your Jars, Lids, and Bands

Because the jar holds the preserve and its mouth should be securely closed, you must inspect the jars, lids, and bands before placing them in the hot water bath canner. The jar's lid should be snug but not overtight.

Before filling, inspect the jar to ensure it is sterilized and clean. The jar size should also be determined by the amount of food to be canned. Also, inspect the jar for any cracks that may have formed. There should be no nicks, chips, or cracks in the canning jar. A cracked jar may result in a poor vacuum, defeating the entire purpose. When canning, inspect the lids and prepare them according to the manufacturer's instructions. Reusing old lids will not provide a sufficient vacuum.

Check For the Most Recent Canning Updates

The canning procedure is updated regularly. If you are very interested in canning, try to stay up to date on any changes in technique or equipment. By staying current on the canning process and tools, you can improve your skills and become an expert in the field. You will make fewer mistakes and be able to complete recipes correctly. Canning equipment and tools are constantly improving as technology and time pass. Begin with beginner's tools, but keep up to date on canning tips and tools.

Choose the Best Ingredients

The entire canning process is focused on preserving the nutritional quality and flavor of the produce or food you can. As a result, for the results to shine, you must select the highest quality ingredients and produce. Your jams, jellies, canned foods, and pickles will only taste good for a long time if you use only the best ingredients. The best way to start a canning process is to use fresh produce from your farm or kitchen garden. When you start with high quality and taste, the final taste of its canned version is also excellent.

Everything Should Be Cleaned

When beginning the canning process, concentrate on preparing the foods, jars, and lids. Clean everything, including the water bath canner, so that the process can be carried out in a sterile manner. Canning foods should be thoroughly cleaned with water and scrubbed. The jars and lids should be sterile and clean as well. This is necessary before canning so that the food does not become contaminated during the process.

Allow the Jars to Cool

When the scanning process is complete, and it is time to remove the jar, use jar lifters to do so carefully. Take care not to damage the jars while removing them. Also, take precautions to avoid being harmed by the heat. Place the jars on a towel or cutting board, leaving enough space between them to allow them to cool evenly. Make sure the jars are completely cool before storing them. Allow the jars to cool completely before proceeding further.

Make Use of Fresh Produce. Avoid Overripe or Bruised Produce

Jars are being overfilled. Make sure there is enough space between the jar's rim and the food's surface.

It will be difficult to properly seal the lids if the jars are nearly full. However, this is not a major issue because you can simply transfer the jar to your refrigerator and use it within a few days or reprocess it with enough head space to adequately seal the jar.

Don't Risk It

If you suspect that food you have canned is bad, do not try to eat it, and just toss it! Each time you open a jar of canned food, inspect it and check for the following:

- Is the lid bulging, swollen, or leaking at all?
- Is the jar cracked or damaged?
- Does the jar foam when opened?
- Is the food inside discolored or moldy?
- Does the food smell bad?

If you notice any of these warning signs in a food that you have canned, throw it away. Do not taste it to check if it is good. It is not worth risking your health to try the food after seeing one of the above signs. Luckily, it is easy to spot a jar of food that has gone bad. Home-canned food can spoil for many reasons. A dent in the lid, a small crack in the jar, an improper seal, or not enough processing time are all common errors that may cause canned foods to go bad. Follow the exact canning directions, and you will never get a bad jar of food!

Thoroughly Read the Recipe

Nothing is more aggravating than getting halfway through a recipe and realizing you're missing a key ingredient. This frustrates me when I'm preparing dinner. It is possible that a dangerous product will be produced when preparing a product for home canning. Most home-canned foods are time-sensitive and cannot be delayed while we look for the right ingredients. So, before you begin, thoroughly read the recipe and gather all of the required ingredients.

Check Over Your Canning Equipment

It's unavoidable: a jar will fracture at some point throughout the canning process. You try to avoid it whenever possible because it's always a mess. Inspect each jar before use for hairline cracks and nicks.

Set aside these jars because they will not withstand a hot water bath. Remove any rusty rings as well. Nobody wants rust in their food, and corroded rings are difficult to screw on. Canners have taken a beating over the years. Check that yours sits flat on the stove and that the cover is positioned properly on top. Examine the region for any spots that have corroded through, allowing water to leak out.

Also, be sure your canner is compatible with your particular stove.

Avoid Botulism

Botulism is an infection caused by the bacteria Clostridium botulinum. The spores of the bacteria thrive in a moist, low-acid, low-oxygen environment, where they produce a lethal toxin. The botulinum toxin cannot be smelled or tasted, yet consuming it can be lethal or cause lasting nerve damage or paralysis.

There should be no botulism worries if you follow the recipe safety recommendations. Botulism cannot flourish in an acidic environment, hence water bath canning is only acceptable for acidic foods. However, be cautious and wash all produce before canning low-acid items such as vegetables, meats, and fish in a pressure canner exclusively. The threat of botulism should not deter you from preserving your produce, but rather urge you to adopt proper safety precautions.

Clean Your Jars and Rings

One way that water bath canning has grown easier over the years is that we no longer need to sterilize jars for most goods. All that remains is to clean the jars, lids, and rings. This indicates that a dishwashing cycle is OK as long as your product has a processing time of at least 10 minutes.

I usually run a cycle right before starting a batch of product so that the jars are clean and warm when the pot of jam or pickles is ready. There are, of course, a few exceptions. Jars that have been treated for less than 10 minutes, such as jelly or fruit curds, must be sterilized before use.

After you've filled the jars, make sure to wipe the rims clean.

Wiping the lips with water or white vinegar prepares the lid's surface for sealing.

Use the Right Headspace

The incorrect amount of headspace might damage a jar of product.

Most pickles necessitate a 12-inch headspace, whereas most jams and soft spreads necessitate only a 14-inch headspace. While in the water bath canner, headspace permits the product to expand.

Processing times are influenced in part by the amount of headspace. As a consequence, it has been discovered that a 15-minute processing period is sufficient for penetrating a quart of pears and driving the residual oxygen out of the jar.

You do not need to be obsessed with it. It's fine if your 12-inch headspace measures 0.53 or 0.48 inches.

A 4-inch headspace, on the other hand, due to a paucity of ingredients (really, I've seen this) will result in a low-quality product.

If you don't have enough ingredients to fill a whole jar, skip the processing and save the jar for later.

Use the Right Headspace

The incorrect amount of headspace might damage a jar of product.

Most pickles necessitate a 12-inch headspace, whereas most jams and soft spreads necessitate only a 14-inch headspace. While in the water bath canner, headspace permits the product to expand.

Processing times are influenced in part by the amount of headspace. As a consequence, it has been discovered that a 15-minute processing period is sufficient for penetrating a quart of pears and driving the residual oxygen out of the jar.

You do not need to be obsessed with it. It's fine if your 12-inch headspace measures 0.53 or 0.48 inches.

A 4-inch headspace, on the other hand, due to a paucity of ingredients (really, I've seen this) will result in a low-quality product.

If you don't have enough ingredients to fill a whole jar, skip the processing and save the jar for later.

Make Sure Your Jars Are Sealed

After the lid has rested, press down on it. A well-sealed lid is one that either stays down or is drawn down by the jar vacuum. Occasionally, 1 or 2 jars in a batch will not seal. If this happens, keep the jars refrigerated until needed, or reheat the product and reprocess the jars.

Never keep an unopened jar of product.

It will spoil quickly, resulting in sickness and waste.

CHAPTER 2
CANNING PROCESS

When you warm up the filled, sealed jars, the contents expand and release steam, which forces air out of the jars. It produces a vacuum seal on the jar as it cools. Sugar content and acidity are two factors that might impact canning and shelf life; it's recommended to start with a canning recipe to determine which technique is appropriate for the food you'll be canning.

In this context, there are two types of food: high and low acid. Each type of food requires a different preparation method to prevent any harmful bacteria growth. Before you even take out the jar, you need to determine the acid level of the food. High-acid foods are those with a pH level of less than 4.6, and you will need a boiling water canner for the job. Here, the natural acid level in the food will kill off any botulism bacteria from making the jar its home, and the heating will also kill most molds, yeasts, and other bacteria that might be present.

On the other end of the spectrum, you have low-acid food that has a pH level of over 4.6, and you will need a pressure cooker. Tomatoes straddle the line between the two food groups, so you should use something acidic like lemon juice or vinegar to make them safe to can up. What if you want to preserve food that is a mixture of high-and low-acid foods? For example, if you want to keep your spaghetti sauce with meat, tomatoes, and veggies, then you should follow the same procedure as preserving low-acid food. As always, when in doubt, look up the specific food you want to preserve.

Filling Jars

Canning experts have recently stated that sterilizing jars and lids is no longer necessary because the water bath process kills any harmful germs. Jars and rings from previous years can be reused if they are in good condition, but new lids are required each time to maintain a good seal. Soak the lids in hot water for at least 10 minutes to soften the rubber edge. When you screw on the rings, the lids will have a better grip on the jar tops.

Jars should be rinsed and dried before filling. Run a load of jars through the dishwasher to clean them all at once. A canning funnel facilitates the filling stage. Fill the jars halfway with ingredients, leaving about an inch at the top for the contents to expand during processing.

The amount of "headspace" required varies by recipe, so read the instructions carefully.

To eliminate air bubbles, run a fine, non-metallic spatula along the insides of the jars after filling, then wash the jar rims with a moist paper towel; any food residue on the rims might inhibit a successful seal. Place the heated lids on the rims and tighten the rings as much as possible, but not too much. Once the jars have cooled, you may tighten the rings even further.

Processing

It's important to make sure that the water level in the kettle is just a little over an inch above the jars' tops. In a kettle, bring water to a boil, then place the jars in a rack into the boiling water and cover it. For most jams, jellies, and chutneys, set a timer for 10 minutes; for fruits and pickles, go by the recipe's directions.

Final Steps

Allow the processed jars to remain undisturbed for at least an hour after removing them from the water bath canner. The lids will get recessed in the middle as the jars cool, and you may hear a small "ping," signaling that the lids have sealed. If they don't seal, either refrigerate the preserved food and eat it within two weeks, or try a different cover and repeat the water bath process. Here you can find some guidelines for safety canning:

Ensuring safe canned foods. Growth of the microorganism and true bacteria in canned foods could cause botulism—a deadly sort of gastrointestinal disorder. These microorganisms exist either as spores or as vegetative cells. The spores that adore plant seeds will survive harmlessly in soil and water for several years. Once ideal conditions exist for growth, the spores turn out vegetative cells that multiply speedily and will turn out a deadly poison inside three to four days of growth in an atmosphere consisting of:
- A moist, low-acid food
- A temperature between 40° and 120°F
- Less than 2 percent oxygen

Beware of Botox

The canning process removes oxygen to prevent the growth of bacteria. The only bacterial exception is the botulinum toxin. It is produced from a spore that can survive without oxygen, like in a vacuum can.

Follow Proper Steps

If the right steps are followed, it is possible canning safely and preserve the quality of the food. Here are the proper canning practices:
- Select and wash fresh food
- Peel some fresh foods
- Hot packing many foods
- Add acids to some foods (lemon juice or vinegar)
- Use suitable jars and self-sealing lids
- Process jars in a boiling-water for the right period

Storing

After you have meticulously prepared and canned your food, there are still a couple of safety practices that you should follow:
- Always label and date all the jars before storage.
- Always put your jars in a place that is dark, cool, and dry.
- Once you pop open a jar for consumption, refrigerate leftovers.
- If you canned seafood and decided to pop it open, refrigerate immediately and throw it out 3 days after opening.
- For the best quality, consume all canned or bottled foods within a year.

Avoiding Spoiling and Avoiding Problems

You're likely to make several blunders that result in poor canning outcomes if you're new to the canning and pickling process. Begin with something simple. If you're new to canning, consider simple items to prepare to prevent problems in the beginning.

After mastering the basics, you may advance to more difficult undertakings like canning and pickling. For a simple first exercise, try preserving tomatoes or making jam.

- **Pick your meal wisely:** Make sure your food is free of mold and discoloration and that your fruit is fresh and ripe. It will improve the canning outcomes and extend the product's shelf life.
- **Decide the technique of canning to use:** Keep in mind that not all items are canned in the same way. Depending on their acidic and pH levels, you choose which approach to utilize.
- **Carefully read the recipe:** Get a hold of some up-to-date canning recipes. Read them thoroughly to ensure that the components are accurate and up-to-date and the quantities. Recipes and procedures for canning have evolved throughout time, and the more modern processes provide superior results.
- **Properly prepare the food:** If the recipes ask for peeling or chopping the ingredients, you should do as precisely as written. Remove any stems, pits, or other inedible pieces to avoid changing the flavor.
- **Wash your hands:** Before preparing the food for canning, wash your hands to prevent germs from entering the food.
- **Clean and sterilize your jars:** Before using them, ensure they have been properly sterilized following the previous use. Disinfect your jars in the dishwasher to sterilize them. Run them through a whole cycle.
- **Leave some headroom at the top:** When filling the jars with food, pack them securely but leave some space at the top. Depending on the sort of food and what the recipe asks for, this may range from 3mm to 25mm.
- **Add preservatives from the start:** Before putting the food into the jar, add the preservative, such as sugar, citric acid, or honey, if you're using one. You do this so that it blends in with the meal when you pour it in.
- **Remove any air bubbles:** remove them at the top by leveling the food with a flat spatula or a knife and ensuring no gaps.
- **Drips and residues:** Wipe out any drips or residues, particularly before sealing the jars.
- **Check the jar seals:** After a few hours, check the seals to make sure the jar contents have drawn the lids down securely. The jars haven't been fully sealed if you can push down on the middle of a lid.
- **General hints:** Once you've opened a jar, keep it refrigerated and use the contents as soon as possible. Make labels for your jars, indicating the contents and the year. If you have a lot of jars, it might be tough to distinguish which ones are which.
- Don't use butter or fat: Unless specifically mentioned in a recipe, don't use butter or fat when canning since they don't preserve well and may cause food deterioration.
- Don't thicken canned foods with starches, flour, barley, pasta, or rice: Even after processing, such food might be dangerous to keep. Thickeners absorb liquid and delay the heating of food.

- **Sprinkle commercially processed ascorbic acid over fresh, ripe, and prepared fruits**: Do this before canning to prevent them from browning. Even cut-up fruit may be soaked in lemon juice. Drain them before putting them in the canner.
- **Unless otherwise noted, use small jars**: Food might be contaminated if jars are larger than required.

Safety Tips

Unfortunately, home canning is not as safe as other hobbies such as knitting or painting. For one, they require special equipment such as metal lids, glass jars, metal rings, pressure cookers, and boiling water canners.

There are also a lot of steps that go into home canning, and there are risks at every step. Therefore, if this is your first time, consider taking a home canning course in addition to reading books on the subject. It is worth getting some practice in a controlled environment, and a classroom allows for just that.

Other than that, there are a couple of safety tips you should follow at each stage of the preparation process. In regards to food preservation, most foodborne illnesses can be avoided if you:
- Wash your hands thoroughly before handling food; ensure all tools and surfaces used are also clean.
- Rinse produce under running water, rubbing the whole surface with your clean hands. Soaps or detergents are not necessary; the friction of the hands loosens bacteria holding dirt and grime, and running water washes it away.
- Don't allow the product to soak. Use sieves, or colanders, for small foodstuffs, and make sure to keep the layers shallowed; so, all surfaces of each bean, berry or other food are rinsed as thoroughly as possible.
- Whether by salting, sugaring, canning, or freezing, food preservation is the art of killing microbes or at least keeping them from reproducing to toxic levels.
- Freezing or refrigerating food keeps bacteria from growing. Unluckily, there are at least two bacteria that can grow at refrigerator temperatures. High salt, sugar, and acid levels also keep bacteria from growing.
- Only heat kills the microbes. If held for even a few seconds, a temperature above 160°F [78°C] is sufficient to kill viruses, parasites, and bacteria, except for one. The bacteria Clostridium produces heat-resistant spores that can only be killed above boiling temperature. Pressure canning produces the high temperature necessary to kill these spores.

Not all toxins produced by bacteria are affected by heat. Therefore, it is very important to preserve always good quality foods. Avoid:

- Split peels or skins
- Bruised fruit
- Evidence of insect attacks
- Nibbles by birds or animals

Ensure all foodstuffs are as fresh as possible and processed in a small, manageable batch as quickly as it can be.

To produce the highest quality preserved foods, you need to process them on the same day as harvest and managing in a sanitary way.

Again, food safety should be your first concern when preserving foodstuffs for future use.

CHAPTER 3
INSTRUMENTS NEEDED
FOR THE CANNING PROCESS

Canning Lids and Screw Bands

The canning lid and the screw band are the two components that together make up a standard canning top. Make sure to get lids compatible with the different kinds of jars you have. Most of the time they are for single use but fortunately don't cost too much. Reusing screw bands or rings is possible, provided they are in excellent condition and do not have any rust. If you want to save even more, you can use some fabric for the jar covers and the string to close them.

Cups for Measuring Liquid

Fruit, vegetables, juice, vinegar, water, and other liquid components may be measured using standard glass liquid cups. Using glasses, ingredients like chili peppers, onions, or liqueurs should be measured.

Dry Measuring Cups

For measuring sugar and other dry ingredients, use a set of graduated plastic or metal dry measuring cups with flat rims. To acquire a precise measurement, you must use measuring cups developed specifically for dry ingredients. The top of this measuring cup is flat-end so that you may level the item with a straight knife or another tool with a straight edge, such as a spatula or bowl scraper.

When using a dry measure, spoon the item into the measuring cup; if you dip the cup into the substance, the ingredient will compress in the cup, resulting in an inaccurate measurement. Nuts and dried fruits may also be measured using dry measuring cups.

Measuring Spoons and Glasses

A set of graduated measuring spoons is essential for measuring tiny amounts of substances. Tiny measuring glasses are useful for measuring small amounts of liquid substances, while they are not required.

Kitchen Timer

Timing is an essential part of canning, too. If you don't want to buy a kitchen timer, you can always use the timer on your phone or tablet. Just make sure you remember to set them when you are cooking and canning.

Zester

A zester is a handy small kitchen gadget with four to six holes that separate colorful zest from citrus fruits in thin, consistent strips, ideal for producing quality marmalades.

Cheesecloth or Bag

When manufacturing jellies, cheesecloth is used to line a sieve to separate the fruit pulp from the juice and filter spices from pickle syrups. Fruit juice may also be strained using a cotton jelly bag. In businesses that sell home canning supplies, jelly bags with metal supports are usually available.

Canner

Canning may be done using either a water bath or under pressure. These are the two primary ways. Pressure canners are far more effective than water bath canners, but using their calls for additional training represents a more significant financial commitment. If you use a large stockpot, you need to make sure that it is big enough to hold at least a couple of inches of water over the jars and have additional space so that the water does not boil over.

Canning Funnel

With a canning funnel, filling jars is much simpler and more orderly than without one. What sets a canning funnel different from a typical funnel used for other purposes? The breadth of the. Wide-mouth funnels, also known as canning funnels, feature a giant hole on the bottom than standard funnels, which makes it much simpler to pour thick sauces or jams into jars.

Jars

The jar is where you put the food that you want to process. There are three parts of a jar: the metal screw band, the metal lid, and the jar. Some types of jars that can be used for food include Mason jars and Ball jars.

You could also use any type of threaded jar that comes with a self-sealing lid. These jars also have a wide opening, approximately three inches, so you can easily empty and fill them.

Jars can come in sizes ranging from ½ a pint up to ½ gallon. They can be reused numerous times until they wear out. You will know that a jar is worn out if it has any type of chip or fraction within the glass. If the jar is even slightly chipped, it will disrupt the seal and possibly break in the canner while you are canning your food.

Canning Rack

If you use a stockpot as a water bath canner, you will need to purchase a second canning rack. Canning racks of various sizes can be purchased online.

Magnetic Lid Grabber

Although sterilizing jar lids before use is no longer required, the lids do need to be clean. Therefore, many of us still warm them in boiling water. This gadget allows you to grip the lid and lift it out of the water, preventing scalded fingers. Tongs may be used to pick up the lids; however, this gadget works like a charm.

Headspace Measuring Tool

Every canning recipe calls for a certain amount of headspace or the space between the top of the container and the lid. This angled tool determines how much headspace you have, allowing you to alter the product amount as needed. The screw rings on the jars normally do the same thing, with the bottom ring showing 12" headspace and the top ring indicating 14" headspace. You can also use a ruler.

Digital Thermometer

If you create a lot of jam and fruit preserves, a candy or deep-fry thermometer can assist you and ensure that you've achieved the gelling point. The boiling point is 8 degrees higher than the gelling point. Other methods, such as the plate technique or the spoon approach (explained here), are less exact but can be used in a hurry. A thermometer ensures that your jams are just right, neither too syrupy nor too thick.

Camp Stove

If you have an older glass-top stove that isn't safe for canning, a camp stove is a must-have.

Even if that isn't an issue, a camp stove may make canning on a hot summer day much more fun. Using a camp stove takes the processing heat out of your kitchen and allows you to spend more time outside enjoying the day.

Cups and Spoons for Measuring

It's essential to use the right measuring cups for measuring the various components in preserved food recipes if you want to have a good canning experience.

Food Mil

A food mill is used to remove seeds and skins from tomatoes for sauces, remove seeds from berries for seedless spreads, and to purée fruits for jars of butter in home canning.

Chopstick or Plastic Knife

Before processing, use a tiny plastic knife or plastic chopstick to coax any trapped bubbles out of jars. Commercial bubble frees are included in some canning equipment sets and may also be bought separately, but they're too big and unwieldy for most varieties of preserves. Use a plastic knife or spoon instead of a metal knife or spoon because metal may damage the jar's interior, causing it to fracture or shatter during heat processing or chilling

The Oven

The oven sterilizing direction is probably the most used technique. Wrap the two shelves in your oven with two layers of newspaper. Ensure there is enough room for the jars around the headspace level, so the glass jar is not touching the top of the oven, and the same goes for the bottom part of the oven. Heat the oven to a maximum heat level of 275°F. If you try to make the oven hotter than the suggested temperature, you will risk the jars breaking in the oven. Put the clean glass jars inside the oven on the shelves. Make sure the jars have their own space and are not touching each other.

Pots and Pans

A large pot is essential because most products must be cooked before canning. A 5-quart saucepan is sufficient for making small batches of jams, pickles, sauces, and other such goods.

However, I recommend that you buy an 8-quart or larger pot or dutch oven. The larger pot reduces the chances of jam or pickles boiling over and spraying you with hot, splattering jam.

It also ensures that all of the ingredients are properly cooked, which adds to the safety of your home-canned product. Instead of aluminum or cast iron, choose enamel, ceramic, or stainless steel. Aluminum and cast iron react with acidic chemicals, leaving your products with a harsh metallic flavor.

Towels

Place tea towels or terrycloth dish towels on the counter to cushion the jars when setting them down. Towels prevent jars from slipping when filling and provide insulation for hot jars after processing. Wipe down the jar lips with a clean towel dipped in water or white vinegar after filling but before installing the two-piece lids. Vinegar is especially useful when canning fatty goods; otherwise, a cloth dampened with water will suffice.

Jar Lifter

A jar lifter is a set of tongs intended to lift jars into and out of a water bath or pressure canner with ease and safety. The lifter keeps a firm grasp on the jar's neck while moving the jar between the counter and the boiling water in the canner. It grabs hot jars and assists you in removing them from the water bath canner. It is a useful instrument and the most effective technique to retrieve hot jars without burning your fingers.

Measuring Spoons and Containers

If you want to have a pleasant canning experience, you must use the proper measuring cups to measure the various components in preserved food recipes. Traditional glass liquid cups can be used to measure fruit, vegetables, juice, vinegar, water, and other liquid components. Because plastic absorbs strong scents from components like chili peppers and onions, I prefer glass measuring cups to plastic. To measure sugar and other dry ingredients, use a set of scales. A set of graded measuring spoons is required for measuring small amounts of substances.

Food Scale

Some individuals believe that a food scale is essential. However, most of the recipes in this book contain ingredient amounts in cups, by number of components, and by weight. When you're not sure how large to cut the fruit or if you have enough goods on hand to create the dish, a food scale might come in helpful. In these cases, use a food scale to weigh the ingredients.

Bubble Remover

This tool is used to eliminate bubbles from full jars and is commonly used while canning fruits and pickles. Any long, nonmetallic device, such as a chopstick, can be used instead, but the bubble remover is thinner and thus easier to use.

Dishwater

You can use this technique only if your dishwater can reach a high temperature. Place the clean jars inside the dishwasher, giving enough adequate space where the glasses are not touching each other. You want to run the dishwasher for as long as it takes you to get your food ready. For instance, if you are canning green beans, then you want to boil the green beans at a high temperature (hot packing), and until your green beans are done, you don't want to take the jars out of the dishwater because your jars will cool down before you get the chance of filling it with the prepped green beans.

Microwave

Microwave the jars on a high setting for 30 to 45 seconds. I would only use this direction for one jar because you want to be sure the heat is distributed equally. Another keynote is to ensure your timing is with whatever food you plan on canning, especially if you are hot packing.

Storage Space

Lastly, you need to ensure you have a storage space to house your canned foods safely. Mason jars can withstand different kinds of situations, but it would be better for you and your cans if you store your canned food in a dry, room-temperature space.

You don't have to erect a shed for storing your jars; it is unnecessarily expensive. You also don't need a bunker to store your jars; that was for back in the day when people's hideaways were required to survive.

You could clear a shelf in your pantry and reserve it for your canned foods. It's as simple as that.

CHAPTER 4: JAMS AND BUTTER

1.

PEACH SPICE JAM

 2 Pint Jar   **Prep Time : 5 Mins**   **Cook Time : 15-25 Mins**

INGREDIENTS

·8 to 9 large peaches pitted

·3 cups sugar

·Juice and rind of ½ lemon

·¼ tsp allspice, optional

·¼ tsp cloves, optional

DIRECTIONS

1. Detach pits and imperfect parts from peaches.
2. In a large kettle, parboil peaches with just enough water to keep them from burning. When peaches are softened, put them through a food mill.
3. To a deep saucepan or cooking pot, attach the peaches and enough water to submerge. Boil until softened. Drain water.
4. Transfer to a blender or food processor. Blend well to make a puree.
5. To the pot or pan, add the puree and other ingredients.
6. Boil the mixture till the thermometer reads 220°F; cook over medium-low heat until firm and thick. Swirl continually to prevent scorching.
7. Spill the hot mixture into pre-sterilized jars directly or with a jar funnel. Keep a headspace of ¼ inch from the jar top.
8. Set a nonmetallic spatula to detach tiny air bubbles and swirl the mixture gently.
9. Wipe the sealing edges. Secure the jars with the lids and adjust the bands/rings to seal and prevent leakage.
10. Set the jars in a cool, dry, and dark place. Allow them to cool down completely.
11. Store in your refrigerator for later use.

NUTRITION

Calories: 435 Kcal

Protein: 5.1g

Carbohydrates: 11.4 g

Fat: 1.4 g

Sugar: 86.3 g

RHUBARB ORANGE JAM

 3-4 Pint Jar   Prep Time : 5 Mins   Cook Time : 45 Mins

INGREDIENTS

· 2 cups white sugar

· 2 tsp grated orange zest

· 2 ½ lb rhubarb, chopped

· ½ cup water

· ⅓ cup orange juice

DIRECTIONS

1. Mix the rhubarb, sugar, orange zest, orange juice, and water in a deep saucepan or cooking pot.

2. Boil the mixture till the thermometer reads 220°F; cook for about 45 minutes over medium-low heat until firm and thick. Stir continually to prevent scorching.

3. Spill the hot mixture into pre-sterilized jars directly or with a jar funnel. Keep a headspace of ¼ inch from the jar top.

4. To detach tiny air bubbles, insert a nonmetallic spatula and stir the mixture gently.

5. Wipe the sealing edges, lose the jars with the lids, and adjust the bands/rings to seal and prevent any leakage.

6. Set the jars in a cool, dry, and dark place. Allow them to cool down completely.

7. Store in your refrigerator for later use.

NUTRITION

Calories: 322 Kcal

Carbohydrates: 23 g

Sugar: 22 g

Protein: 15 g

Fat: 2.1 g

3.

BLACKBERRY JAM

 10 Pint Jar   **Prep Time : 15 Mins**   **Cook Time : 30 Mins**

INGREDIENTS

·5 cups blackberries
·2 cups sugar
·2 tbsp lemon juice

DIRECTIONS

1. Sterilize the bottles in a water bath canner. Allow the bottles to cool.
2. Place all ingredients in a saucepan. Set to a boil while constantly stirring for 10 minutes. Reduce the heat to simmer until the sauce thickens.
3. Set off the heat and allow it to cool slightly.
4. Transfer the mixture to sterilized bottles and remove the air bubbles. Close the lid.
5. Set in a water bath canner and process for 10 minutes.
6. Consume within a year.

NUTRITION

Calories: 196 Kcal   Carbohydrates: 49.7 g   Sugar: 44.9 g

Protein:1.7 g   Fat: 0.2 g

HONEYBERRY JAM

🥣 **6.5 Pint Jar** ✕ **Prep Time : 15 Mins** **Cook Time : 25 Mins**

INGREDIENTS

·2 cups honeyberry fruit

2 cups sugar

DIRECTIONS

1.   Sterilize the bottles in a water bath canner. Allow the bottles to cool.

2.   Place all ingredients in a saucepan. Macerate the berries using a potato masher or a ladle.

3.   Turn on the heat to medium-high and bring to a boil while stirring constantly. Reduce the medium-low heat and allow to simmer for another 15 minutes or until the mixture thickens.

4.   Set off the heat and allow the mixture to cool slightly.

5.   Transfer the mixture to sterilized bottles and remove the air bubbles. Close the lid.

6.   Bring in a water bath canner and process for 10 minutes.

7.   Consume within a year.

NUTRITION

Calories: 190 Kcal   Carbohydrates: 48.9 g   Sugar: 47.4 g

Protein: 0.3 g   Fat: 0.01 g

5.

BLUEBERRY VANILLA JAM

 22 Pint Jar   Prep Time : 15 Mins   Cook Time : 22 Mins

INGREDIENTS

- 6 large canning bottles
- 1 ¼ lb blueberries, rinsed and stems removed
- ¾ cup granulated sugar
- 2 tbsp lemon juice
- ½ vanilla bean pod, seeds scraped
- 1 tsp pectin

DIRECTIONS

1. Sterilize the bottles in a water bath canner. Allow the bottles to cool.
2. Place all ingredients except pectin in a pot and mash until the blueberries are macerated.
3. Set on the heat and bring to a boil for 10 minutes while stirring constantly. Remove the vanilla bean pod and stir in the pectin. Continue stirring for another 2 minutes until the mixture becomes thick.
4. Ladle into the sterilized jars and leave ¼ inch of headspace. Remove the air bubbles and screw the lid on.
5. Place in a water bath canner and follow the general instructions for water bath canning.
6. Process for 10 minutes.
7. Consume within a year and keep refrigerated once the bottles are opened.

NUTRITION

Calories: 38 Kcal   Carbohydrates: 9.2 g   Sugar: 8.7 g

Protein: 0.19 g   Fat: 0.2 g

LEMON HONEY MARMALADE

12 Pint Jar	Prep Time : 10 Mins	Cook Time : 40 Mins

INGREDIENTS

- 8 cups lemons, chopped
- 6 oz liquid pectin
- 1 ½ cup water
- 4 cups erythritol
- 2 cups honey

DIRECTIONS

1. Add lemons, erythritol, water, and honey in a saucepan and bring to a boil over medium heat.
2. Reduce heat and simmer for 30 minutes.
3. Add pectin and boil for 5 minutes. Stir constantly.
4. Remove pan from heat. Ladle the marmalade into the jars. Leave ½-inch headspace. Remove air bubbles.
5. Seal jars with lids and process in a boiling water bath for 10 minutes.
6. Remove jars from the water bath and let them cool completely.

Check the seals of jars. Label and store

NUTRITION

Calories: 468 Kcal	Fat: 0.4 g	Sugar: 0 g
Cholesterol: 0 mg	Carbohydrates: 127.5 g	Protein: 1.7 g

7.

CARROT PINEAPPLE PEAR JAM

 8.5 Pint Jar　 Prep Time : 5 Mins　 Cook Time : 45 Mins

INGREDIENTS

- 20 oz crushed pineapple, undrained
- 1 ½ cup peeled, shredded carrots
- 1 ½ cup ripe, peeled, chopped pears
- 3 tbsp lemon juice
- 1 tsp ground cinnamon
- ¼ tsp ground cloves
- ¼ tsp ground nutmeg
- 1 package powdered fruit pectin
- 6 ½ cups sugar

DIRECTIONS

1. In a medium saucepan, bring the first 7 ingredients to a boil.
2. Reduce heat to low and cook, covered, for 15-20 minutes, or until pears are cooked, stirring occasionally.
3. Add pectin. Bring to a full boil, stirring constantly.
4. Stir in sugar. Boil and stir for 1 minute.
5. Remove from heat and skim off the foam.
6. Scoop the heated mixture into half-pint jars that have been sterilized, leaving a 14-inch gap at the top. Remove any air bubbles and, if necessary, correct the headspace with the hot mix. Wipe the rims with a soft cloth. Screw on bands until fingertip tight. Place caps on jars and screw on bands until fingertip tight.
7. Fill the canner halfway with hot water, ensuring the jars are completely submerged. Allow 10 minutes for the water to boil. Remove the jars and set them aside to cool.

NUTRITION

Calories: 88 Kcal　　　Total Carbohydrates: 23 g

Total Fat: 0 g　　　　　Proteins: 0 g

GREEN TOMATO JAM

 3.5 Pint Jar Prep Time : 10 Mins Cook Time : 20 Mins

INGREDIENTS

- 2 ½ cups pureed green tomatoes
- 2 cups sugar
- 1 package of raspberry gelatin

DIRECTIONS

1. Bring the sugar and tomatoes to a boil in a large saucepan.
2. Reduce heat to low and cook for 20 minutes, uncovered.
3. Remove the pan from the heat and stir in the gelatin until it dissolves completely.
4. Skim off any foam.
5. Scoop the heated mixture into half-pint sterilized jars, leaving a 14-inch gap at the top. Remove any air bubbles and, if necessary, correct the headspace with the hot mix. Wipe the rims with a soft cloth. Allow cooling completely before covering with lids. Keep refrigerated for up to 3 weeks.

NUTRITION

Calories: 81 Kcal

Total Carbohydrates: 20 g

Total Fat: 0 g

Proteins: 1 g

9.

PLUM JAM

 4.5 Pint Jar   **Prep Time : 15 Mins**   **Cook Time : 30 Mins**

INGREDIENTS

- ½ cup lemon juice
- ½ cup water
- 3 cups of sugar
- 3 lb plums, halved, pitted, and quartered

DIRECTIONS

1. In a large saucepan, combine everything and bring to a boil to dissolve sugar, stirring continuously for 20 minutes or until the gelling point is reached.

2. Remove from heat and ladle jam into jars, leaving ¼ inch headspace. Process jars for 10 minutes. Remove your jars and let them cool for 12 hours before consumption or storage.

NUTRITION

Calories: 49 Kcal   Carbohydrates: 13 g

Fat: 0 g   Protein: 0 g

STRAWBERRY RHUBARB JAM

🥣 **4.5 Pint Jar**   ✂️ **Prep Time : 15 Mins**   🕐 **Cook Time : 70 Mins**

INGREDIENTS

- 1 tbsp lemon juice
- 2 ¼ cups sugar
- 2 strawberries, hulled, halved
- 5 cups rhubarb, cubed

DIRECTIONS

1. In a saucepan, combine everything over medium heat. Once bubbling, reduce to medium-low heat. It should bubble, but not violently when stirred.
2. Stir occasionally until thickened. Cook for an hour at 205°F. Ladle jam into jars leaving ¼ inch headspace.
3. Process jars for 10 minutes. Remove your jars and let them cool for 24 hours before consumption or storage.

NUTRITION

Calories: 61 Kcal	Fats: 8 g
Carbohydrates: 15 g	Protein: 14 g

GRAPE JELLY

 4 Pint Jar   **Prep Time : 15 Mins**   **Cook Time : 10 Mins**

INGREDIENTS

- 4 cups white (granulated) sugar
- 3 cups grape juice
- 1 packet pectin
- 2 tbsp lemon juice
- 1 tbsp butter

DIRECTIONS

1. Put the grape juice, butter, pectin, and lemon juice into your preserving pan. Bring to a rolling boil on high heat, stirring continuously.

2. Boil for one minute. Stir in the sugar and pectin and keep stirring until it has dissolved. Return to the boil and boil for a minute, still stirring

3. Remove from heat and test the setting point. When the setting point has been achieved, skim scum and jar.

NUTRITION

Calories: 40 Kcal   Fat: 0 g

Carbohydrates: 10 g   Protein: 0 g

SPIKED PEACH JAM WITH GINGER

5.5 Pint Jar | **Prep Time : 25 Mins** | **Cook Time : 30 Mins**

INGREDIENTS

- 4½ cups peeled peaches, finely chopped
- 4 tbsp lemon juice
- 3 cups white sugar
- 1 tsp ground ginger
- 1 (1.75 oz) package of light pectin
- ⅓ cup amaretto liqueur

DIRECTIONS

1. To keep peaches from browning, place them in a glass or plastic box with a cover and add lemon juice right away. Combine the sugar and ginger in a mixing bowl. Cover and marinate for 8 hours overnight in a cool location.

2. Examine 5 half-pint jars for fractures and corrosion on the rings, and eliminate any that are unsatisfactory. Place in a pot of simmering water until the jam is ready. In warm soapy water, wash fresh, unused lids and rings.

3. Transfer the peaches and any remaining liquid to a large saucepan. Stir in the pectin and gently bring the mixture to a full rolling boil, stirring constantly. Cook for 1 min while continually stirring.

4. Remove from the heat and mix in the amaretto liqueur, tasting as you go.

5. Fill the prepared jars with peach jam to within ¼ inch of the top. To eliminate any air bubbles, run a knife or thin spatula along the insides of the jars.

6. To remove any spillage, wipe the rims with a wet paper towel. Cover with lids and secure with rings.

7. Fill a big stockpot partly with water and place a rack in the bottom. Bring to a boil, then use a holder to drop jars 2 inches apart into the hot water.

8. More boiling water should be added to cover the jars by at least 1 inch. Bring to a boil, then reduce to a simmer for 10 minutes.

9. Take the jars from the stockpot & arrange them several inches apart on a cloth-covered or wood surface.

10. Allow yourself a 24-hour rest period without moving. To guarantee that the lids do not slide up or down, gently push the center of each lid with your finger.

11. Remove the rings and keep them in a cold, dark location.

NUTRITION

Calories: 70.1 Kcal	Protein: 0.2 g
Carbohydrates: 17 g	Fat: 0.1 g

13.

SAVORY PEACH JAM PRESERVE

 8 Pint Jar   **Prep Time : 10 Mins**   **Cook Time : 30 Mins**

INGREDIENTS

·10 cups peaches chopped

·5 cups sugar

·3 tsp lemon juice

DIRECTIONS

1. To begin, grab your glass bowl and add the peaches, sugar, and lemon juice one by one.
2. Gently combine the ingredients. Allow approximately 60 to 70 minutes for the peaches to soak up the sugar.
3. Pour the peach mixture into a saucepan and cook over medium heat.
4. Allow the peach mixture to simmer for approximately 5 minutes.
5. Increase the heat to high, stir gently, and cook for approximately 20 minutes, or until the sugar has fully melted.
6. Remove it from the fire after that. Do not pour the hot preserves straight into the jars. Allow 15 to 20 minutes for cooling.
7. Finally, gently fill the pre-sterilized jars.
8. Seal the jars' tops with waxed discs, then cover them with elastic bands & cellophane or lids.
9. Allow the jars to cool completely before labeling them. Store in a cool, dry location.

NUTRITION

Calories: 651 Kcal	Protein: 17 g
Carbohydrates: 93 g	Fat: 26 g

PINEAPPLE & MARASCHINO CHERRY JAM

 7 Pint Jar | Prep Time : 10 Mins | Cook Time : 15 Mins

INGREDIENTS

- 1 orange, large size
- 3 cups chopped pears cored
- ¾ cup pineapple, crushed & drained
- 5 cups sugar
- ¼ cup maraschino cherries chopped
- ¼ cup lemon juice
- 1 pack of 3 oz powdered pectin

DIRECTIONS

1. Begin by peeling the orange and chopping the pulp.
2. To prepare the jam, combine the pineapple, pears, lemon juice, pectin, cherries, and pulp in a saucepan.
3. Keep the heat on high and wait a few minutes for the mixture to heat up.
4. Finally, whisk in the sugar and let it dissolve fully.
5. Remove it from the heat and use a spoon to remove the froth.
6. Fill the jars with the fruity jam mixture and set them in the pre-sterilized jars.
7. Keep the jam in a dry, cold place and enjoy it.

NUTRITION

Calories: 690 Kcal | Protein: 21 g

Carbohydrates: 114 g | Fat: 19 g

15.

TRIPLE BERRY SPICED JAM

 10 Pint Jar   Prep Time : 30 Mins   Cook Time : 25 Mins

INGREDIENTS

- 6 cups sugar
- 4 cups crushed strawberries
- 2 cups crushed blueberries
- 2 cups crushed raspberries
- 2 tbsp shredded lemon peel
- ½ cup lemon juice
- 1 tsp ground cinnamon

DIRECTIONS

1. Combine sugar, blueberries, crushed strawberries, raspberries, lemon juice, and lemon peel in a 6-to 8-quart heavy saucepan. Over medium heat, bring to a boil, constantly stirring to dissolve the sugar.

2. Cook, stirring regularly, for 25 to 30 minutes, uncovered until the mixture sheets off a metal spoon. Stir in the cinnamon until it's well blended.

3. Fill half-pint canning jars halfway with hot jam, leaving ¼-inch headspace. Adjust lids & screw bands after wiping jar rims.

4. In a boiling-water canner, a process filled jars for 10 minutes (when water returns to boiling).

5. Remove the jars from the canner and place them on wire racks to cool. This recipe makes 10 half-pints.

NUTRITION

Calories: 37 Kcal   Protein: 0 g

Carbohydrates: 10 g   Fat: 0 g

BLACKBERRY JALAPEÑO JELLY

 4.5 Pint Jar   **Prep Time : 30 Mins**   **Cook Time : 10 Mins**

INGREDIENTS

- 1 (1.75 oz) powdered pectin, package
- 4 cups blackberry juice
- 1 green jalapeno pepper
- 1 red jalapeno pepper
- 3½ cups white sugar
- 5 half-pint jars for canning with lids & rings

DIRECTIONS

1. In a bowl, combine the pectin crystals &½ cup sugar. In a saucepan, combine the pectin mixture, blackberry juice, green jalapeño, & red jalapeno; bring to a high boil for 1 minute.

2. Return to a rolling boil and cook for 1 minute, or until the sugar has completely dissolved. Eliminate from heat and whisk for around 5 minutes to remove bubbles and froth.

3. Fill sterilized jars with the mixture, allowing ¼ inch headspace.

4. In a hot water bath, seal the jars.

5. After the seal is broken, keep the jelly refrigerated.

NUTRITION

Calories: 43.1 Kcal   Protein: 0 g

Carbohydrates: 11.1 g   Fat: 0 g

17.

APRICOT LAVENDER JAM

 8.5 Pint Jar   Prep Time : 30 Mins   Cook Time : 5 Mins

INGREDIENTS

- 4½ cups white sugar
- 1 tbsp dried lavender blossoms
- 3½ lb fresh apricots, sliced and pitted
- 2 tbsp lemon juice
- 1 (1.75 oz) package of fruit pectin
  (Pectin light, no sugar)

DIRECTIONS

1. In the bowl of a food processor, combine ½ cup sugar & lavender flowers; pulse till the lavender blossoms are finely diced, and the sugar is aromatic.

2. Measure the apricots; you should have around 5 cups of ready-to-eat fruit. Place in a plastic or glass jar with a tight-fitting cover and chop coarsely. Combine the lavender sugar & lemon juice in a mixing bowl. Refrigerate overnight, covered.

3. Inspect 8 half-pint jars for fractures and corrosion on the rings, and reject any that are unsatisfactory. Place in a pot of simmering water until the jam is ready. In warm soapy water, wash fresh, unused lids and rings.

4. In a dish, combine ¼ cup leftover sugar and pectin; pour over apricots. Mix the fruit mixture well in a big pot. Bring to a high rolling boil, occasionally stirring, until it stops bubbling. To thoroughly dissolve the sugar, add the rest sugar and stir well, scraping the bottom of the pan. Cook for 1 minute while continually stirring.

5. Pour the apricot jam into the prepared jars as soon as possible, filling them to within ¼ inch of the surface. To eliminate any air bubbles, run a good knife or thin spatula along the insides of the jars. To remove any spillage, wipe the rims with a wet paper towel. Cover with lids and secure with rings.

6. Fill a big stockpot partly with water and place a rack in the bottom. Bring to a boil, then use a holder to drop jars 2 inches apart into the hot water. More boiling water should be added to cover the jars by at least 1 inch. Bring to a boil, then reduce to a simmer for 10 minutes.

7. Take the jars from the stockpot & arrange them several inches apart on a cloth-covered or wood surface. Allow for a 24-hour rest period without moving the jars. To guarantee that the lids do not slide up or down, gently push the center of each lid with your finger. Remove the rings and keep them in a cold, dark location.

NUTRITION

Calories: 33 Kcal	Protein: 0.2 g
Carbohydrates: 8.4 g	Fat: 0 g

BALSAMIC VINEGAR RUBY PORT JELLY

 4.5 Pint Jar   Prep Time : 30 Mins   Cook Time : 10 Mins

INGREDIENTS

·⅓ cup balsamic vinegar

·¼ cup coarsely orange peel shredded

·3 cups sugar

·2 cups ruby port

·½ of a 6-oz package of liquid fruit pectin

DIRECTIONS

1. Combine the orange peel and vinegar in a small saucepan. Bring to a boil, then turn off the heat. Cover and cook for 3 to 5 minutes, or until the vinegar has been reduced to ¼ cup.

2. Remove the pan from the heat. Cover and set aside to cool. Using a fine-mesh screen, strain the mixture; discard the peel.

3. Combine the sugar, reduced vinegar, and port in a 4- to 6-quart heavy saucepan. Over high heat, bring to a full rolling boil, stirring frequently. Stir in the pectin quickly.

4. Return to a high rolling boil, continually stirring. Cook for 1 minute on high heat, stirring regularly. Remove the pan from the heat. With a metal spoon, quickly skim off the froth.

5. Fill half-pint canning jars halfway with heated jelly, leaving ¼-inch headspace. Adjust lids & screw bands after wiping jar rims.

6. Place the jars in a water bath for 10 minutes.

7. Remove the jars from the canner and place them on wire racks to cool. This recipe makes 4 half-pints.

NUTRITION

Calories: 50 Kcal   Protein: 0.2 g

Carbohydrates: 11 g   Fat: 0.1 g

19.

CAYENNE TOMATO JAM

 4 Pint Jar   **Prep Time : 20 Mins**   **Cook Time : 30 Hours**

INGREDIENTS

· 4 lb tomatoes, peeled & chopped

· 1 apple, peeled & chopped

· 1 cup raw sugar

· 1 diced yellow onion

· ½ cup brown sugar

· ¼ cup apple cider vinegar

· 3 tbsp lemon juice

· 1 tsp salt

· ½ tsp ground cayenne pepper

DIRECTIONS

1. In a large saucepan, bring the apple, tomatoes, sugar, brown sugar, onion, lemon juice, apple cider vinegar, salt, and cayenne to a boil. Reduce heat to low and cook, stirring periodically, for approximately 2 hours 30 minutes, or until black and syrupy.

2. Continue to boil for another 30 minutes or until the mixture thickens to a jam-like consistency. Remove the jam from the heat and set aside to cool for 1 to 2 hours. Refrigerate after transferring to closed containers.

NUTRITION

Calories: 52 Kcal   Protein: 0.6 g

Carbohydrates: 12.9 g   Fat: 0.1 g

GINGER PEAR FREEZER JAM

 7.5 Pint Jar   **Prep Time : 30 Mins** 🕐 **Cook Time : 10 Mins**

INGREDIENTS

- 5½ cups (fresh, peeled, chopped) pears
- 1 package pectin
- 1½ tsp grated lemon zest
- 2 tbsp lemon juice
- 1 tsp fresh (minced ginger root)
- 4 cups sugar
- 1 tsp vanilla extract

DIRECTIONS

1. Combine the pears, lemon juice, pectin, lemon zest, and ginger in a Dutch oven. Bring to a rolling boil, continually stirring. Add the sugar and mix well. Allow boiling for 1 minute while continually stirring. Pour in the vanilla extract. Remove the pan from the heat and skim off the foam.

2. Fill hot sterilized 1-cup containers halfway with the hot mixture, leaving a 14-inch gap at the top. Remove any air bubbles and adjust the headspace as needed by adding hot mix. Wipe the rims with a soft cloth. Put the tops on. Allow around 24 hours for the jam to set.

NUTRITION

Calories: 64 Kcal   Fat: 0 g

Carbohydrates: 17 g   Protein: 0 g

21.

STOVETOP APPLESAUCE

 4 Pint Jar   Prep Time : 10 Mins   Cook Time : 25 Mins

INGREDIENTS

- 3 lb apples
- ½ cup water or apple juice
- 2 tbsp sugar or 1½ tbsp honey, optional
- 2 tbsp lemon juice

DIRECTIONS

1. Apples should be cleaned before eating. If you have one, you can deal with the peels afterward using a food mill or food processor. If you don't want to peel the apples, peel them beforehand. Remove the cores. Apples should be cut into 1-inch thick slices. Add the apples to a large saucepan half-filled with water. Sugar should be sprinkled on the apples, while honey should be dissolved in the water. Combine the lemon juice and water in a saucepan. Cook for 20 to 25 minutes over medium heat, occasionally stirring, until the apples are soft. To remove the peels from the applesauce, put it through a food mill or purée it in a food processor. If you peeled the apples, mash them with a potato masher or purée them in a blender or food processor. Applesauce may be stored in the refrigerator for up to a week or frozen for 6 months.

2. Fill clean, heated pint or half-pint jars halfway with applesauce, leaving 12 inches of headspace for extended storage at room temperature. When filling the jars, the applesauce should still be warm. Before filling the jars with applesauce that has already cooled or been in the refrigerator for a couple of days, could you bring it to a boil over medium heat? Remove any air bubbles from the insides of the filled jars using a table knife. Clean the jar rims with a damp cloth. Put on the canning lids and cook for 20 minutes in a boiling water bath.

NUTRITION

Calories: 86 Kcal	Fat: 0 g
Carbohydrates: 21 g	Protein: 0 g

CLASSIC BLUEBERRY JAM

 1 Pint Jar   Prep Time : 5 Mins   🕐 Cook Time : 15 Mins

INGREDIENTS

- 2 ¾ cups sugar
- 2 tbsp Sure-Jell
- 25 oz (5 cups) of blueberries
- 2 tbsp bottled lemon juice
- 1 tsp grated lemon zest

DIRECTIONS

1. In a big saucepan, lay a canning rack, 4 1-cup jars, and enough water to cover by 1 inch. Over medium heat, bring to a simmer, then remove from heat and cover to keep warm. In a mixing dish, combine 14 cups of sugar and Sure-Jell. In a Dutch oven over medium-high heat, bring blueberries, lemon juice, and lemon zest to a simmer. Reduce heat to medium-low and cook, stirring periodically, for approximately 5 minutes, until blueberries have softened and released their juice. Over high heat, bring the mixture to a boil. Bring the Sure-Jell mixture to a boil, whisking constantly.

Bring to a boil, whisking in the entire 21/2 cup of sugar. Cook for 1 minute, whisking regularly after the water has to a boil. Remove the saucepan from the heat and use a spoon to remove any foam from the surface of the jam. Place a flat dishtowel on the counter. Remove jars from the saucepan using a jar lifter, emptying water into the pot. Allow 1 minute for jars to dry upside down on the towel. Fill heated jars with hot jam using a funnel and ladle, allowing a 14-inch headspace. To eliminate air bubbles, run a wooden skewer around the inner edge of the jar and draw upward.

2. While the jars are still hot, wipe the rims clean, add the lids, and screw on the rings until fingertip-tight; do not overtighten. Bring the kettle of water with the canning rack back to a boil. Lower the jars into the water, cover them, and bring the water back to a boil before starting the timer. The amount of time it takes to cook depends on your altitude:

- Boil for 10 minutes up to 1,000 feet
- 15 minutes between 1,001 and 3,000 feet
- 20 minutes between 3,001 and 6,000 feet
- 25 minutes between 6,001 and 8,000 feet

3. Turn off the heat and set aside the jars in the saucepan for 5 minutes. Remove the jars from the saucepan and set them aside to cool for 24 hours. Remove the rings, inspect the seal, and clean the rims. (You may keep sealed jars for up to a year.)

NUTRITION

Calories: 64 Kcal	Fat: 0 g
Carbohydrates: 17 g	Protein: 0 g

23.

FIG AND PEAR JAM

 4 Pint Jar   **Prep Time : 20 Mins**   **Cook Time : 30 Mins**

INGREDIENTS

- 2 cups chopped pears
- 2 cups fresh figs
- 4 tbsp Pectin
- 2 tbsp lemon juice
- 1 tbsp water
- 3 cups sugar

DIRECTIONS

1. Combine all ingredients except the sugar in a 4-quart (4-L) stainless steel. Over high heat, bring the mixture to a boil that cannot be stirred down, stirring frequently.

2. Stir in the sugar until it dissolves. Bring the mixture back to a full boil. 1 minute of vigorous boiling, stirring continually. Remove the pan from the heat. If necessary, skim the foam. Fill a heated jar halfway with hot jam, leaving a 14-inch (5-cm) headspace. Wipe the jar's rim. On the jar, place the lid in the middle. Apply the band and tighten it until it is fingertip-tight. In a boiling-water canner, place the jar. Rep until all of the jars are full.

3. Adjust for altitude and process jars for 10 minutes. Remove jars from heat, remove lids, and set aside for 5 minutes. Remove the jars and set them aside to cool.

NUTRITION

Calories: 76 Kcal	Fat: 0 g
Carbohydrates: 15 g	Protein: 0 g

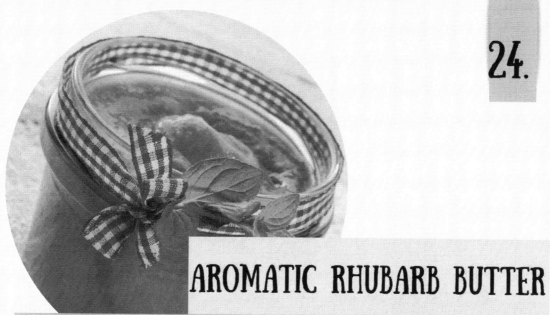

AROMATIC RHUBARB BUTTER

 2 Pint Jar   Prep Time : 15 Mins Cook Time : 50 Mins

INGREDIENTS

- 4 cups rhubarb, chopped
- 2 tbsp water
- Juice of 1 lemon
- ½ cup sugar
- Seeds of 1 vanilla bean

DIRECTIONS

1. Combine all the ingredients in a heavy-bottomed pan over medium heat. The rhubarb will release its juices. Simmer for 20 to 30 minutes or until the fruit is soft, stirring to ensure it doesn't stick.

2. Puree the thick butter to desired consistency and return to the pot and simmer for 20 minutes until thick then scoop into storage jars. Tightly seal and refrigerate or process for canning.

NUTRITION

Calories: 18 Kcal	Total Fat: 0 g	Dietary Fiber: 1.3 g	Protein: 0 g
Cholesterol: 0 mg	Carbohydrates: 2.7 g	Sugars: 3 g	Sodium: 0 mg

25.

LAVENDER-INFUSED APRICOT BUTTER

 2 Pint Jar | Prep Time : 15 Mins | Cook Time : 60 Mins

INGREDIENTS

- 25 apricots, peeled, chopped, and pitted
- 3 tbsp freshly squeezed lemon juice
- 2 ½ tbsp lavender buds (food grade)
- 3 cups white sugar
- ½ cup water

DIRECTIONS

1. Tightly wrap the lavender buds in a cheesecloth. Add the water and apricots to a large pot and place over medium to high heat. Add in the wrapped lavender buds and bring to a boil. Bring to a simmer and let cook until the apricots become soft and the lavender flavor is to your liking.

2. Remove from heat and use an immersion blender to blend the apricots to desired texture. Mix in the sugar and lemon juice and return to heat until it starts boiling gently. Lower the heat and continue stirring to ensure it doesn't burn. Turn off the heat when the butter starts sticking to the spoon.

3. For canning, prepare a hot water bath and scoop the butter into the prepared jars and seal tightly. Process for 15 minutes then move to a cool and dry place.

NUTRITION

| Calories: 96 Kcal | Total Fat: 0 g | Dietary Fiber: 0.8 g | Protein: 0 g |
| Cholesterol: 0 mg | Carbohydrates: 26 g | Sugars: 33 g | Sodium: 1.9 mg |

26.

CINNAMON
PEAR & APPLE BUTTER

🥣 **1 Pint Jar** | 🍴 **Prep Time : 15 Mins** | 🕐 **Cook Time : 4 Hours**

INGREDIENTS

- 3 pears, sliced
- 3 large apples, sliced
- 1 cup apple juice
- 1 tsp vanilla extract
- 2 tsp cinnamon
- ¼ cup honey

DIRECTIONS

1. In a pan, combine apple juice, pears, and apples; cook for about 1 ½ hour or until pears and apples are tender.

2. Stir in vanilla, cinnamon, and honey, and cook for another 2 hours.

3. Remove from heat and mash the mixture into a smooth paste. Let cool and then blend in a blender until smooth.

4. Return to heat and cook for 30 minutes. Transfer to sterile jars and seal.

5. Process for at least 30 minutes in a hot water bath.

NUTRITION

Calories: 43 Kcal	Total Fat: 0.1 g	Dietary Fiber: 1.4 g	Protein: 0.2 g
Cholesterol:0 mg	Carbohydrates: 11.2 g	Sugars: 8.8 g	Sodium: 1 mg

27.

TASTY PASSION BUTTER

 2 Pint Jar   Prep Time : 10 Mins   Cook Time : 30 Mins

INGREDIENTS

· 2 cups strained passion
fruit pulp with a few seeds,
optional
· 1 tbsp freshly squeezed
lemon juice
· 1 cup butter (dairy or
vegan), chopped
· ¾ cup sugar
· 3 free-range eggs
· 2 free-range egg yolks

DIRECTIONS

1. Combine the first 4 ingredients in a large pan over medium heat and cook until the butter melts and the sugar dissolves, then remove from heat.

2. Whisk the eggs and yolks until very well beaten, then whisk into the butter mixture, without stopping. Return to heat and reduce to low and continue cooking while stirring until the butter becomes thick for about 5 to 7 minutes.

Let the butter cool before scooping it into storage jars and refrigerating.

NUTRITION

Calories: 61 Kcal	Carbohydrates: 26 g	Sugars: 3 g	Cholesterol: 31 mg
Total Fat: 2 g	Dietary Fiber: 1.3 g	Protein: 6 g	Sodium: 317 mg

TART BERRY APPLE BUTTER

🥣 **2 Pint Jar**   ✕ **Prep Time : 10 Mins**   🕐 **Cook Time : 150 Mins**

INGREDIENTS

- 6 Granny Smith apples, chopped and cored
- 1 cup fresh cranberries
- ½ cup water
- 1 cinnamon stick
- Raw honey, adjust to taste

DIRECTIONS

1. Combine the apples, cranberries, and water in a crockpot and cook on high for 2 to 3 hours, occasionally stirring to prevent sticking. Blend the fruit mixture to desired consistency and pass through a sieve, optional, to get rid of the cranberry skins. Return to the crockpot and add the cinnamon stick. Cook uncovered until you get butter that's thick to your desire. Taste to gauge the sweetness and add raw honey, if desired.

2. Scoop into storage jars, cover tightly, and refrigerate or process for canning.

NUTRITION

Calories: 22 Kcal	Total Fat: 0 g	Dietary Fiber: 1.3 g	Protein: 0 g
Cholesterol: 0 mg	Carbohydrates: 2.3 g	Sugars: 3 g	Sodium: 1mg

29.

AMAZING APPLE BUTTER

 6 Pint Jar   **Prep Time : 10 Mins**   **Cook Time : 10 H 25 Mins**

INGREDIENTS

- ·10 lb apples, quartered
- ·4 cups unsweetened apple juice
- ·1 cup white sugar
- ·1 tbsp apple cider vinegar
- ·1½ tsp ground cinnamon
- ·½ tsp ground cloves
- ·½ tsp ground allspice
- ·6 half-pint canning jars with lids and rings

DIRECTIONS

1. In a stockpot, combine the apples & apple juice and bring to a boil. Reduce heat to low and cook for 20 to 30 minutes, or until apples are soft and mushy.

2. Place the apples in a food mill & purée them, eliminating the cores and skins that remain in the mill. Place the apples in a slow cooker once they have been processed.

3. Cook on high for 12 to 24 hours, with the lid open, till the humidity evaporates & the volume is reduced by roughly half.

4. Mix the apple puree with the apple cider vinegar, sugar, cinnamon, cloves, & allspice.

5. Cook on High for another 2 to 5 hours, or until the mix mounds on a cooled platter without any water breaking from the borders.

6. Boil the jars & lids for at least 5 minutes to sterilize them. Fill the heated, sterilized jars with apple butter, filling them to within ¼ of the top.

7. To eliminate any air bubbles, run a blade or a small spatula along the inside of the bottles after they've been filled.

8. To eliminate any food residue, wipe the jar rims with a wet paper towel. Screw on the rings and cover with lids.

9. Fill a big stockpot partly with water and place a shelf at the bottom. Bring to a boil, then use a holder to drop the jars into the hot water. Make sure there's a 2-inch gap between the jars. If required, add extra boiling water to elevate the water level to at least 1" over the jar tops. Raise water to a boil, then cover and cook for 10 minutes.

10. Remove the bottles from the large pan and set them several inches apart on a fabric or wood surface to cool. Once cool, squeeze the top of each lid with your finger to ensure a firm seal. Keep it in a cold, dark place.

NUTRITION

Calories: 75 Kcal	Protein: 0.3 g
Carbohydrates: 19.7 g	Fat: 0.2 g

PLUM BUTTER

 4 Pint Jar Prep Time : 10 Mins 🕐 Cook Time : 6 H 45 Mins

INGREDIENTS

·4½ lb plums, pitted and diced

·¼ cup water, or as needed

·1 cup white sugar

DIRECTIONS

1. Place plum in a large pan with just enough liquid to cover the bottom; simmer over very low flame, stirring regularly, for approximately 2 hours, or until plums are broken down. Remove the stockpot from the heat and set it aside to cool for 2 hours.

2. Place the stockpot on the burner over low heat and simmer for 3 hours, stirring occasionally. Remove from the heat and set aside for 8 hours to overnight at room temperature.

3. Cook plums for 2 hours over low flame, stirring periodically. Remove from the fire and set aside for 2 hours to cool.

4. Brought plum to a boil. Sugar should be added, reduced heat, and simmer for 15 minutes or until thickened.

5. Boil the jars and lids for at least 5 minutes to sterilize them. Fill heated jars with plum butter to within ¼ of the top. To eliminate any air bubbles, run a clean blade or thin spatula along with the interior of the jars. To eliminate any food residue, wipe the jar rims with a wet paper towel. Lids and rings are screwed on top.

6. Fill a big stockpot partly with water and place a shelf at the bottom. Bring to a boil, then use a holder to drop the jars into the hot water. Make sure there's a 2-inch gap between the jars. If required, add extra boiling water to elevate the water level to at least one inch over the jar tops. Raise water to a boil, then cover and set aside for 15 minutes.

7. Remove the bottles from the large pan and set them several inches apart on a fabric or wood surface to cool. With your finger, press down on the top of each lid to ensure firm closure. Keep it in a cold, dark place.

NUTRITION

Calories: 54 Kcal	Protein: 0.4 g
Carbohydrates: 13.5 g	Fat: 0.2 g

31.

MAPLE BLACKBERRY JAM

 6 Pint Jar   **Prep Time : 15 Mins**   **Cook Time : 60 Mins**

INGREDIENTS

·6 canning bottles

·6 cups blackberries, crushed

·1 ½ cup pure maple syrup

·Zest and juice from one
lemon

DIRECTIONS

1. Sterilize the bottles in a water bath canner. Allow the bottles to cool.
2. Set all ingredients in a saucepan and bring to a simmer. Cook for 50 minutes while stirring constantly over medium-low heat or until the mixture thickens.
3. Dip an old spoon into the jam and tip gently. If it runs off in a sheet and if the liquid does not drip, the jam is ready.
4. Set off the heat and allow the mixture to slightly cool before transferring it into the sterilized bottles.
5. Remove the air bubbles in the mixture. Close the lid and place it in the water bath canner.
6. Process for 10 minutes.
7. Store in a cool dark place and consume within a year.

NUTRITION

Calories: 379 Kcal   Carbohydrates: 96 g   Sugar: 84.2 g

Protein: 2.9 g   Fat: 0.4 g

PINEAPPLE JAM

 4 Pint Jar Prep Time : 15 Mins 🕐 Cook Time : 70 Mins

INGREDIENTS

·2 canning bottles

·1 cup sugar

·2 fresh lemons, juiced

·1 medium-sized pineapple, peeled and chopped

DIRECTIONS

1.Sterilize the bottles in a water bath canner. Allow the bottles to cool.

2.Add all ingredients to a medium-sized pot and bring to a boil. Reduce the heat and simmer for an hour until the liquid has evaporated and the mixture thickens.

3.Set off the heat and allow it to slightly cool before transferring it into the bottles.

4.Remove the air bubbles and close the lid.

5.Set in a water bath canner and process for 10 minutes.

Consume within a year.

NUTRITION

Calories: 216 Kcal	Carbohydrates: 56.3 g	Sugar: 47.3 g
Protein: 1.3 g	Fat: 0.3 g	

65

33.

CHERRY JAM

🥣 **4 Pint Jar** ✕ **Prep Time : 15 Mins** 🕐 **Cook Time : 60 Mins**

INGREDIENTS

·4 canning bottles
·2 lb cherries, stems removed
and pitted
·2 ½ cups sugar
·1 lemon juice, freshly squeezed
·2 drops of almond extract

DIRECTIONS

1.Sterilize the bottles in a water bath canner.
Allow the bottles to cool.
2.Place all ingredients in a saucepan and cook for
40 minutes or until the mixture thickens.
Continue swirling to prevent the bottom from
burning.
3.Turn off the heat and remove from the pot to
slightly cool.
4.Transfer to the bottles. Remove the air bubbles
and close the lid.
5.Set in a water bath canner and process for 10
minutes.
6.Consume within a year.

NUTRITION

Calories: 331 Kcal	Carbohydrates: 83.6 g	Sugar: 78.7 g
Protein: 1.9 g	Fat: 0.6 g	

RASPBERRY JAM

 6 Pint Jar **Prep Time : 15 Mins** **Cook Time : 30 Mins**

INGREDIENTS

·4 canning bottles with lid

·4 cups crushed ripe raspberries

·1 tbsp fresh lemon juice

·6 ½ cups sugar

·½ tsp unsalted butter

·3-oz pectin

DIRECTIONS

1. Sterilize the bottles in a water bath canner. Allow the bottles to cool.
2. Macerate the raspberries and run through a colander to remove the seeds.
3. Place the strained raspberries in a pot and stir in the lemon juice, sugar, and butter.
4. Set the heat to medium and bring to a rolling boil for 10 minutes. Reduce the heat to simmer for 5 minutes before adding the pectin. Allow to simmer for another 2 minutes.
5. Turn off the heat to cool.
6. Transfer the jam to sterilized bottles and remove the air bubbles.
7. Close the lid.
8. Bring in a water bath canner and process for 10 minutes.
9. Consume within a year.

NUTRITION

Calories: 581 Kcal	Carbohydrates: 148 g	Sugar: 5.9 g
Protein: 1.4 g	Fat: 0.4 g	

67

35.

APPLE PIE JAM

 8 Pint Jar   Prep Time : 15 Mins   Cook Time : 30 Mins

INGREDIENTS

- ·6 canning bottles
- ·4 cups diced apples
- ·2 tbsp lemon juice, freshly squeezed
- ·1 ¼ tsp ground cinnamon
- ·¼ tsp ground ginger
- ·¼ tsp ground nutmeg
- ·4 cups granulated sugar
- ·1 cup packed brown sugar
- ·½ tsp unsalted butter
- ·1 box pectin

DIRECTIONS

1. Sterilize the bottles in a water bath canner. Allow the bottles to cool.
2. Place the apples, lemon juice, cinnamon, ginger, nutmeg, sugar, and butter in a saucepan.
3. Turn on the heat and allow simmering for 15 minutes. Stir in the pectin and simmer for 2 minutes. Keep swirling to avoid the mixture from burning.
4. Turn off the heat to cool.
5. Transfer the mixture to sterilized bottles and remove the air bubbles. Close the lid.
6. Set in a water bath canner and process for 10 minutes.
7. Consume within a year.

NUTRITION

Calories: 275 Kcal   Carbohydrates: 70.6 g   Sugar: 66.9 g

Protein: 0.2 g   Fat: 0.3 g

STAR FRUIT JAM

 6 Pint Jar   **Prep Time : 15 Mins**   **Cook Time : 30 Mins**

INGREDIENTS

·2 canning bottles

·1 ¼ lb carambolas or star fruit, edges trimmed and chopped

·1 cup water

·2 cups white sugar

1 lemon juice, freshly squeezed

DIRECTIONS

1.Sterilize the bottles in a water bath canner. Allow the bottles to cool.

2.Place all ingredients in a saucepan. Set on the heat and bring the mixture to a simmer. Stir for 20 minutes or until the mixture is thick and the liquid has reduced.

3.Set off the heat and allow the mixture to cool down.

4.Transfer the mixture to sterilized bottles and remove the air bubbles. Close the lid.

5.Bring in a water bath canner and process for 10 minutes.

6.Consume within a year.

NUTRITION

Calories: 241 Kcal   Carbohydrates: 60.3 g   Sugar: 54.6 g

Protein: 1.5 g   Fat: 0.5 g

69

37.

NECTARINE BROWN SUGAR JAM

 8 Pint Jar   **Prep Time : 15 Mins**   **Cook Time : 25 Mins**

INGREDIENTS

·6 to 8 canning bottles

·4 lb nectarines, peeled, seeded, and chopped

·1 ½ cup brown sugar, lightly packed

·4 tbsp lemon juice

·½ tsp cinnamon

·¼ tsp ground ginger

DIRECTIONS

1.Sterilize the bottles in a water bath canner. Allow the bottles to cool.

2.Place all ingredients in a big saucepan and bring to a rolling boil for 5 minutes. Set the heat to low and parboil for another 10 minutes. Keep stirring until the mixture thickens.

3.Set off the heat and allow it to cool slightly.

4.Transfer the mixture to sterilized bottles and remove the air bubbles. Close the lid.

5.Bring in a water bath canner and process for 10 minutes.

6.Consume within a year.

NUTRITION

Calories: 259 Kcal   Carbohydrates: 65.2 g   Sugar: 58.1 g

Protein: 2.5 g   Fat: 0.8 g

STRAWBERRY JAM

🥣 **4 Pint Jar** 🍴 **Prep Time : 15 Mins** 🕐 **Cook Time : 80 Mins**

INGREDIENTS

- 2 pints jar
- 2 lb ripe strawberries, hulled and cleaned
- 2 ½ cups sugar
- 1 tbsp freshly squeezed orange juice

DIRECTIONS

1. Sterilize the bottles in a water bath canner. Allow the bottles to cool.
2. Chop the strawberries and place all ingredients in a large pan. Let it sit for an hour until the sugar dissolves and the mixture becomes watery.
3. Heat over the stove using a medium flame and bring to a boil. Make sure to stir constantly and mash with the ladle to macerate. Cook for 10 minutes then let cool.
4. Place the strawberry jam in sterilized bottles.
5. Set in a water bath canner and process for 10 minutes.
6. Consumer within a year.

NUTRITION

Calories: 318 Kcal	Carbohydrates: 80.2 g	Sugar: 73 g
Protein: 1.6 g	Fat: 0.7 g	

CHAPTER 5: MAIN FOODS

39.

CHICKEN WITH GARLIC

 3   **Prep Time : 20 Mins**   **Cook Time : 90 Mins**

INGREDIENTS

- ·1 crushed garlic clove
- ·3 skinless, boneless chicken breasts
- ·½ tsp sea salt
- ·½ tsp black pepper
- ·Water, as needed

DIRECTIONS

1. Put part of the garlic clove at the bottom of each sanitized quart jar.
2. Add chicken pieces, pushing them down to pack tightly.
3. Add salt and pepper, and then fill the jar with water, allowing 1 inch of headspace.
4. Carefully slide a rubber spatula down the interior sides of the jars, removing air pockets. Do not skip this step, or your jars may not seal. Wipe the rims of the jars.
5. Process in a pressure canner for 90 minutes at 10 PSI, adjusting for altitude with the lids on.

NUTRITION

Calories: 233.1 Kcal	Fat: 8.3 g	Protein: 27.9 g
Cholesterol: 0 mg	Carbohydrates: 8.6 g	Sugar: 0 g

74

SOY MARINATED SALMON JERKY

🍜 2   **Prep Time : 20 Mins**   ⏲ **Cook Time : 4 Hours**

INGREDIENTS

- 1 lb boneless salmon fillet
- ¼ tsp salt
- ½ cup apple cider vinegar
- 2 tbsp low-sodium soy sauce
- ¼ tsp black pepper
- 1 tbsp fresh lemon juice
- 2 tsp paprika
- ½ tsp garlic powder

DIRECTIONS

1. Freeze the salmon for about 30 minutes until it is firm.
2. Meanwhile, whisk together the apple cider vinegar, soy sauce, and lemon juice in a mixing bowl.
3. Add the paprika and garlic powder, then stir well.
4. Season the salmon with salt and pepper to taste, then remove the skin.
5. Slice the salmon into ¼-inch thick strips, then place them in a bowl or glass dish.
6. Pour in the marinade, turning to coat, and then cover with plastic and chill for 12 hours.
7. Drain the salmon slices and place them on paper towels to soak up the extra liquid.
8. Spread the salmon slices on your dehydrator trays in a single layer.
9. Dry for 3 to 4 hours at 145°F (63°C) until dried, but still tender and chewy.
10. Cool the salmon jerky completely, then store it in airtight containers in a cool, dark location.

NUTRITION

Calories: 203 Kcal	Protein: 20 g	Carbohydrates: 27 g
Cholesterol: 0 mg	Fat: 5 g	Sugar: 0 g

41.

GINGER MISO SALMON SALAD

 2   **Prep Time : 20 Mins**   **Cook Time : 10 Mins**

INGREDIENTS

- 2 tbsp white miso paste
- 1 tbsp brown sugar
- 1 tsp grated ginger
- 1 tbsp low sodium soy sauce
- 4 oz salmon fillet
- 2 shredded carrots
- ½ cup edamame
- ½ diced cucumber
- 8 cups chopped romaine
- ¼ cup roasted peanuts

DRESSING

- 2 tbs price wine vinegar
- 1 tbsp sesame oil

DIRECTIONS

1. Preheat the oven to 350°F.
2. Mix the miso paste, sugar, ginger, and soy sauce in a small bowl until well combined.
3. Put the salmon fillet on a baking sheet and drizzle half the miso mixture over the fish.
4. Transfer the salmon to the oven for 8 to 10 minutes, or until cooked. Remove from the oven for cooling.
5. Break the salmon into large flakes using a fork once cooled.
6. To make the dressing, incorporate the rice wine vinegar and sesame oil into the remaining miso mixture. Spoon equal amounts of the dressing into 2 quart-sized canning jars.
7. Pile on the rest of the ingredients in the following order: carrots, edamame, cucumber, salmon, romaine lettuce, and peanuts.
8. Cover with the lids, and you are ready to go.

NUTRITION

Calories: 424 Kcal	Fat: 25 g	Protein: 37 g
Cholesterol: 0 mg	Carbohydrates: 30 g	Sugar: 7.08 g

CANNED TUNA

🥣 3   ✕ **Prep Time : 20 Mins**   **Cook Time : 20 Mins**

INGREDIENTS

- ·3 lb tuna
- ·2 cups water
- ¼ tsp salt

DIRECTIONS

1. After removing the viscera, wash the fish thoroughly and drain out all blood.

2. Slice the tuna into crosswise halves. Add salt Bake at 250°F for 4 hours, and then put in the refrigerator to allow the meat to firm up.

3. Remove the skin, blood vessels, discolored/dark flesh, fin bases, and bones. Slice into quarters and add to clean and hot Mason jars, packing firmly in oil or water. Make sure an inch of headspace remains and that all air bubbles are removed from the jars.

4. Adjust the lids and place them in the pressure canner. Process for 1 hour and 20 minutes.

NUTRITION

Calories: 104 Kcal	Sodium: 33 mg	Fat: 4.1 g	Protein: 1.3 g
Cholesterol: 0 mg	Dietary Fiber: 1.4 g	Carbohydrates: 16.3 g	Sugar: 0 g

43.

FISH CHOWDER

 8   **Prep Time : 20 Mins**   **Cook Time : 30 Mins**

INGREDIENTS

- ¾ cup chopped onion
- 3 tbsp butter
- ½ cup chopped celery
- 2 cups diced potatoes
- 1 tsp garlic powder
- 2 cups chicken broth
- 2 diced carrots
- 1 tsp black pepper
- 1 tsp salt
- 32 oz canned fish
- 1 tsp dried dill weed
- 15 oz canned creamed corn
- 12 oz. canned evaporated milk
- ½ lb shredded cheddar cheese

DIRECTIONS

1. In a pot over medium heat, melt butter.
2. Cook celery, onion, and garlic powder for 5 minutes in the melted butter.
3. Stir in carrots, potatoes, salt, broth, pepper, and dill.
4. Boil, then reduce the heat to low.
5. Cover and simmer for 20 minutes.
6. Stir in milk, cheese, corn, and fish.
7. Cook until the cheese melts.
8. Fill jars with fish chowder to ½ inch from the top.
9. Put the jars in the canner and fill them with water up to the jar rings.
10. Close and lock the pressure canner and bring it to a boil over high heat, then add cooking weight to the top.
11. After 20 minutes, turn the heat to medium and cook for 75 minutes.
12. Turn off the heat and leave the canner alone until it has cooled completely to room temperature.
13. After the canner has cooled, remove the jars from the canner and check for sealing.
14. If the jars have been sealed, store them for up to 2 years; if not, use the meat immediately.

NUTRITION

Calories: 249.0 kcal	Fat: 8.1 g	Protein: 26.5 g
Cholesterol: 0 mg	Carbohydrates: 14.5 g	Sugar: 0 g

BLACK-EYED PEAS WITH PORK

🍜 2   **Prep Time : 20 Mins**   🕐 **Cook Time : 90 Mins**

INGREDIENTS

·2 lb chopped pork

·3 lb dried black-eyed peas

·6 crushed cloves garlic

·2 cups diced green bell pepper

·2 cups diced tomato

·2 chopped onions

·1 diced jalapeño pepper

·Hot water, as needed

DIRECTIONS

1.   Layer the ingredients in each of your jars in the order listed, leaving 1 inch of headspace.

2.   Add hot water over the contents of the jars, allowing 1 inch of headspace for the peas to expand.

3.   Use a rubber utensil to slide around the edges of the jar to remove air pockets. Add more liquid if necessary.

4.   Put in a pressure canner at 10 PSI for 90 minutes with lids on, adjusting for altitude.

NUTRITION

Calories: 860 Kcal	Fat: 70 g	Protein: 52 g
Cholesterol: 0 mg	Carbohydrates: 1 g	Sugar: 0 g

45.

TERIYAKI BEEF JERKY

 2 **Prep Time : 20 Mins** **Cook Time : 4 Hours**

INGREDIENTS

- 3 lb boneless beef sirloin
- ¼ tsp salt
- ¼ cup low-sodium soy sauce
- ¼ tsp black pepper
- ¼ cup light brown sugar, packed
- 2 tbsp liquid smoke
- 1 tsp cider vinegar

DIRECTIONS

1. Whisk together the soy sauce, sugar, liquid smoke, and cider vinegar in a mixing bowl.
2. Trim the fat from the beef and cut it into ¼-inch thick strips.
3. Rub the beef with seasonings, to taste, then add to the bowl with the marinade.
4. Toss to coat, then cover with plastic and chill for 24 hours.
5. Spread the meat slices on your dehydrator trays in a single layer.
6. Dry for 4 hours at 145°F (63°C) until dried but still tender and chewy.
7. Cool the jerky completely, and then store it in airtight containers in a cool, dark place.

NUTRITION

Calories: 298 Kcal	Carbohydrates: 32 g	Protein: 24 g
Cholesterol: 0 mg	Fat: 11 g	Sugar: total 0.72 g

BUTTERED CHICKEN BREAST

| 8 Pints | Prep Time : 15 Mins | Cook Time : 90 Mins |

INGREDIENTS

·18 medium boneless and skinless chicken breasts

·1 ½ tbsp salt

·4 ½ cups of water

·Butter or olive oil for frying in the skillet

DIRECTIONS

1. Cook each side of the chicken in a skillet with some butter or olive oil, for about 8 to 10 minutes. Remove from the heat when the chicken is white and cooked all the way through. If you poke it with a fork, the juices should run clear.

2. In each pint jar, place ½ tsp salt and 2 chicken breasts. Fill the jar with water.

3. Can for 70 minutes at 10 lb pressure for the weighted gauge of the pressure canner or 11 lb if the pressure canner has a dial gauge.

4. Remove the jars, and let them cool until it is at room temperature, which may take about a day.

NUTRITION

Calories: 45 Kcal

Carbohydrates: 0 g

Fat: 1 g

Protein: 9 g

47.

CHICKEN AND POTATO

🥣 **6 Pints**   ✂️ **Prep Time : 15 Mins**   🕐 **Cook Time : 90 Mins**

INGREDIENTS

- 2 tbsp butter
- 4 cubed chicken breasts
- 4 cubed chicken thighs
- 1 chopped onion
- 6 minced garlic cloves
- 6 cups potatoes
- 8 cups divided chicken broth
- ½ cup ClearJel
- 2 tbsp distilled white vinegar

DIRECTIONS

1. In a sizable skillet, heat the butter over medium-high heat. Add the chicken, onion, and garlic, and cook for 10 minutes, stirring occasionally.

2. Arrange the hot jars on a cutting board. Evenly distribute the cooked chicken mixture among the jars.

3. Next, evenly distribute the potatoes among the jars, being sure to leave a generous 1-inch headspace.

4. In the same skillet, add 6 cups of chicken broth and bring to a boil over high heat.

5. In a small bowl, whisk the ClearJel with the remaining 2 cups of broth until well distributed. Add the mixture to the broth as you stir, then boil for another minute.

6. Arrange the hot jars on a cutting board. Using a funnel, ladle the hot gravy into the jars, leaving 1-inch headspace.

7. Remove any air bubbles and add additional gravy if necessary to maintain the 1-inch headspace. Rinse the rim of each jar with a warm washcloth dipped in distilled white vinegar and seal the lids.

8. Pour 3 quarts of water into the pressure canner and add 2 tbsp distilled white vinegar. Arrange the jars in the pressure canner and bring them to a boil over high heat while locked.

9. Vent the pressure canner for 10 minutes. Seal the vent and keep heating to reach 11 PSI for a dial gauge and 10 PSI for a weighted gauge. Can for 90 minutes (quarts) and 75 minutes (pints).

NUTRITION

Calories: 296.2 Kcal	Carbohydrates: 34.6 g	Protein: 24 g
Fat: 6.3 g	Protein: 23.6 g	Sugar: total 0.72 g

BEEF CUBES

🥣 **7 Pints** **Prep Time : 15 Mins** **Cook Time : 100 Mins**

INGREDIENTS

- ·5lb beef stew meat
- ·1 tbsp vegetable oil
- ·12 cups cubed potatoes
- ·8 cups sliced carrots
- ·3 cups chopped celery
- ·3 cups chopped onion
- ·1 ½ tbsp salt
- ·1 tbsp thyme
- ·½ tbsp pepper
- ·Water to cover

DIRECTIONS

1. Brown the meat in a large saucepot with some oil. Add the vegetables and all seasonings, then cover with water. Boil the stew and remove it from the heat.

2. Scoop the hot stew into hot quart jars. Leave a 1-inch headspace. If needed, remove air bubbles to adjust the headspace, then rinse the rims of the jars with a paper towel, dampened and clean.

3. Now apply the 2-piece metal caps. Can the quart jars in a pressure canner for about 90 minutes at 11 lb pressure if using a dial-gauge canner or 10 lb pressure if using a weighted-gauge canner.

NUTRITION

Calories: 877 Kcal	Carbohydrates: 59.2 g
Fat: 22.6 g	Protein: 104.6 g

49.

CHICKEN TACO MEAT FOR PRESSURE CANNING AND POTATO

 7 Quarts   Prep Time : 30 Mins   Cook Time : 90 Mins

INGREDIENTS

- ·14 lb chicken
- ·1 large onion
- ·4 poblano peppers
- ·1 ½ tbsp kosher salt
- ·3 tbsp garlic powder
- ·1 tbsp ground cumin
- ·2 tbsp onion powder
- ·3 tbsp chili powder
- ·2 tbsp Mexican oregano
- ·1 to 2 tsp cayenne pepper
- ·2 cups Chicken broth or filtered water

DIRECTIONS

1. In hot, soapy water, wash the jars, lids, and rings. Fill the pressure canner with water according to the instructions on your computer.
2. Combine the onions, chicken, peppers, and all of the spices and herbs in a large mixing bowl. Uniformly coating
3. Remove any air bubbles and leave 1-inch headspace in the jars. If necessary, add a little cold water or cold chicken broth to get a 1-inch headspace. Wipe rims and fingertip-tighten lids and rings. Cold jars should be placed in a cold canner.
4. Process for 90 minutes for quarts and 75 minutes for pints.

NUTRITION

Calories: 12 Kcal	Protein: 9 g
Carbohydrates: 3 g	Fat: 8 g

STRONG FISH STOCK

| 4 Quarts | Prep Time : 15 Mins | Cook Time : 45 Mins |

INGREDIENTS

- 8 medium carrots
- 4 medium onions
- 4 tbsp unsalted butter
- 8 stalks celery
- 2 tbsp black peppercorns
- ½ cup dry white wine
- 4 bay leaves
- 12 to 16 sprigs of fresh thyme
- 8 lb fish bones
- 4 quarts hot water
- A pinch of kosher salt

DIRECTIONS

1. Prepare the veggies by slicing the onions crosswise into thin slices. Carrots should be peeled, and celery should be sliced.
2. In a large 12–16 quart stockpot, melt the butter. Cook, stirring periodically, until the veggies soften without browning, add the onions, carrots, celery, bay leaves, parsley, thyme, and peppercorns. This might take anything from 10 minutes.
3. Arrange the fish frames on top of the veggies in an equal layer. Pour in the wine, cover, and let aside for 15 to 20 minutes, or until the bones have gone fully white.
4. Stir in the heated water and bring to a gentle simmer over high heat. Reduce heat to low and cook for 10 minutes, stirring occasionally. Remove from the fire, give it a quick stir, and set aside for 15 minutes.
5. Using a fine strainer, strain the stock; season with a pinch of salt. Cool and chill the stock if you aren't intending to can it right away. The stock may be frozen or kept in the refrigerator for up to 3 days.

NOW TO PRESSURE CAN THE FISH STOCK:

1. Start using clean, hot jars in the preparation. Check your jars for nicks, and don't use any jars that are defective for canning. They should be clean but not sterile. If you're beginning with hot soup, start with hot jars plus hot water in the canner; if the temps are consistent, you won't lose jars to thermal shock.
2. Keep a supply of clean jar bands on hand. Put clean lids inside a dish and cover with boiling water; set aside until ready to use.
3. Fill the pressure canner halfway with water (usually marked on the inside.) I prefer to add a tbsp of white vinegar to this water to prevent a film from forming on my jars after they've been canned. Heat the water to the point where it will be hot when the heated jars are placed in it.
4. Bring the fish stock to a low boil. Fill heated jars halfway with stock, allowing one inch of headspace. Apply the bands after wiping the rims and centering the hot lids on the jars. Fingertip-tighten the bands; they shouldn't be turned on too hard.
5. Jars at 10 lb pressure for 30 minutes (pints) or 35 minutes (quarts)— altitude adjustments may be necessary. Allow the canner to cool and restore to zero lb pressure for itself after the timer has expired. Remove the jars to a towel-lined surface and let them aside for 24 hours before checking the lids for an appropriate seal. When the center is squeezed, the lids should not bend up and down.
6. Make sure the jars are labeled.

NUTRITION

Calories: 23 Kcal	Protein: 3 g
Carbohydrates: 0 g	Fat: 1 g

51.

MINESTRONE SOUP

🥣 4   🍴 **Prep Time : 10 Mins**   🕐 **Cook Time : 12 Mins**

INGREDIENTS

- ¼ cup dehydrated corn
- ¼ cup dehydrated bell peppers
- ¼ cup dehydrated carrots
- ¼ cup dehydrated peas
- ¼ cup dehydrated green beans
- ¼ cup dehydrated sliced onion
- ¼ cup dehydrated celery
- ¾ cup pasta
- 1 tbsp dried beef bouillon
- 1 tsp dried parsley
- ½ tsp Italian seasoning
- ¼ cup tomato powder
- 6 cups water
- osher salt
- 3 tbsp garlic powder
- 1 tbsp ground cumin
- 2 tbsp onion powder
- 3 tbsp chili powder
- 2 tbsp Mexican oregano
- 1 to 2 tsp cayenne pepper
- 2 cups Chicken broth or filtered water

DIRECTIONS

1. Add all ingredients except water into the glass jar. Seal the jar tightly with a lid and shake well.

2. To cook: Add water and jar content to the saucepan and bring to a boil.

3. Reduce heat and simmer for 12 minutes or until vegetables and pasta are cooked.

4. Serve and enjoy.

NUTRITION

Calories: 128 Kcal	Fat: 1 g	Carbohydrates: 28.1 g
Cholesterol: 0 mg	Protein: 3.6 g	Sugar: 0 g

CHICKEN BROTH

🍜 2   ✕ Prep Time : 10 Mins   🕐 Cook Time : 45 Mins

INGREDIENTS

·Chicken carcass bones, meat removed

·2 quartered onions, optional

·2 sliced celery stalks, optional

·2 bay leaves, optional

·Salt to taste water to cover, optional

DIRECTIONS

1. Place the chicken bones and all optional ingredients in a stockpot, large, then add water to cover everything.

2. Cover the pot and simmer for about 30 to 45 minutes until the remaining meat tidbits fall off easily.

3. Remove and discard the bones, then strain the broth and discard bay leaves and vegetables.

4. Cool the broth, then skim off the fat and discard it. Season with salt if desired.

5. Reheat your broth to boiling.

6. Scoop broth into quart jars. Leave a 1-inch headspace.

7. Wipe the jar rims using a clean damp paper towel, then apply the 2-piece metal caps.

8. Process the quart jars in a pressure canner for 25 minutes at 11 lb pressure if using a dial-gauge canner, or at 10 lb pressure if using a weighted-gauge canner.

NUTRITION

Calories: 233 Kcal	Fat: 13.1 g	Protein: 16.5 g
Cholesterol: 0 mg	Carbohydrates: 12.1 g	Sugar: 4.9 g

53.

CHICKEN TORTILLA SOUP

 6 **Prep Time : 10 Mins** **Cook Time : 12 Mins**

INGREDIENTS

- ·1 cup dehydrated chicken
- ·¼ tsp ground chipotle pepper
- ·1 cup dried corn
- · cup dried green chilies
- ·½ cup dehydrated sliced onion
- ·1 tsp garlic powder
- ·2 tsp chicken bouillon
- ·1 ½ tbsp chili powder
- ·½ cup tomato powder
- ·8 cups water

DIRECTIONS

1. Add all ingredients to the glass jar. Seal the jar tightly with a lid and shake well.
2. To cook, add water and jar content to the saucepan and bring to a boil.
3. Reduce heat and simmer for 15 to 20 minutes.
4. Serve with tortilla chips.

NUTRITION

Calories: 120 Kcal	Fat: 1.6 g	Carbohydrates: 19.2 g
Cholesterol: 0 mg	Protein: 9.8 g	Sugar: 0 g

WHITE BEANS & CORN CHILI

| 🥣 8 Pints | 🍴 Prep Time : 15 Mins | 🕐 Cook Time : 40 Mins |

INGREDIENTS

- 1lb white beans, soaked for 6 hours and drained
- 6 cups chicken broth
- 1-lb frozen corn
- 1 medium onion, chopped
- 7 oz canned green chilies
- 6 garlic cloves
- 4 tsp ground cumin
- 1 tsp dried oregano
- 2 tsp cayenne pepper

DIRECTIONS

1. In a Dutch oven, add beans and enough water to cover over high heat and cook until boiling. Adjust the heat to low and cook for about 30 minutes. Drain the beans completely and set aside.

2. In 7 (1-pint) hot sterilized jars, divide the beans. Fill each jar with hot broth mixture, leaving a 1-inch space from the top.

3. Run your knife around the insides of each jar to remove any air bubbles. Wipe any trace of food off the rims of jars with a clean, moist kitchen towel.

4. Close each jar with a lid and screw on the ring. Carefully place the jars in the pressure canner and process at 10 lb pressure for about 75 minutes.

5. Remove the jars from the pressure canner and place them onto a wood surface several inches apart to cool completely.

6. After cooling with your finger, press the top of each jar's lid to ensure that the seal is tight. Store these canning jars in a cool, dark place.

NUTRITION

Calories: 166 Kcal   Carbohydrates: 28.3 g

Fat: 2.1 g   Protein: 11.4 g

55.

CHICKEN AND SPINACH SALAD

🥣 2   Prep Time : 20 Mins   Cook Time : 0 Mins

INGREDIENTS

· 8 oz cooked and chopped chicken breast
· 2 cups halved grapes
· cup chopped walnuts
· cup shaved Parmesan
· 4 cups baby spinach

DRESSING

· 2½ tsp red wine vinegar
· 2½ tsp country dijon mustard
· ¼ tsp salt
· ½ tsp chopped thyme
· ¼ tsp black pepper
· 2½ tbsp extra virgin olive oil

DIRECTIONS

1. Whisk together the vinegar, mustard, thyme, salt, and pepper in a small bowl. Add the oil into the mixture while constantly stirring until the mixture emulsifies.
2. Divide the dressing equally between 2 quart-sized canning jars. Place the chicken chunks at the bottom of the container and layer in the grapes, walnuts, cheese, and roughly torn spinach leaves.
3. Cover with the lids, and you are ready to eat on the go!

NUTRITION

Calories: 461 Kcal	Fats: 27 g	Protein: 47 g
Cholesterol: 0 mg	Carbohydrates: 22 g	Sugar: 0 g

CHICKEN CACCIATORE

🥣 8   🍴 **Prep Time : 20 Mins**   🕐 **Cook Time : 20 Mins**

INGREDIENTS

- ·3 tbsps olive oil
- ·8 boneless and skinless chicken breasts, cubed
- ·12 boneless and skinless chicken thighs, cubed
- ·1 tbsp dried oregano
- ·1 tbsp dried basil
- ·1 tsp dried thyme
- ·1 tsp dried rosemary, crushed
- ·1 tsp coarse sea salt
- ·½ tsp ground black pepper
- ·1 cup red wine
- ·4 cups diced tomatoes, with their juice
- ·4 cups tomato juice
- ·2 cups sliced white mushrooms
- ·3 cups coarsely chopped sweet onion
- ·1 chopped red bell pepper
- ·1 chopped celery stalk
- ·6 minced garlic cloves
- ·¾ cup tomato paste
- ·1 tbsp granulated sugar

DIRECTIONS

1. In a thick-bottomed stockpot, combine the oil and the chicken thighs and breasts.
2. Mix well to coat the chicken. Cook the chicken for 3 minutes on medium-high heat as you stir often.
3. Add the seasonings, thyme, oregano, basil, and rosemary.
4. Mix evenly and cook for an additional 3 minutes.
5. Add the red wine and cook for 5 minutes while covered.
6. Add the tomatoes, celery, onion, mushrooms, bell pepper, tomato juice, and garlic.
7. Mix well and allow to boil for 5 minutes.
8. Stir in the sugar and tomato paste and cook for another 5 minutes, then remove from the fire.
9. Fill each hot jar ¾ full with the chicken and veggies.
10. Add the hot tomato sauce over the mixture, leaving some space.
11. Remove any air bubbles and add more sauce if necessary.
12. Rinse the rim of each jar with a warm washcloth dipped in distilled white vinegar, then tighten the lids.
13. Arrange the jars in the pressure canner with the lids on.
14. Allow the canner to vent for 10 minutes, then close the vent and continue heating to attain 10 PSI for a weighted gauge and 11 PSI for a dial gauge.
15. Can the quart jars for 1 hour 30 minutes and pint jars for 1 hour 15 minutes.

NUTRITION

Calories: 701 kcal	Carbohydrates: 42.14 g	Protein:37.12 g
Cholesterol: 0 mg	Fat: 43.8 g	Sugar: 11.35 g

57.

WHOLE CHICKEN

 3   **Prep Time : 20 Mins**   **Cook Time : 20 Mins**

INGREDIENTS

- 1 tsp salt in each quart
- 32 cups water
- 1 whole chicken, cut into pieces
- 3 bay leaves
- 6 cups chopped carrots
- 3 cups diced Roma tomatoes
- 4 celery stalks with the leaves, chopped (2 cups)
- 2 cups diced onions
- 8 chopped garlic cloves
- 1 tbsp dried basil
- 1 tbsp coarse sea salt, optional
- 2 tsp ground black pepper

DIRECTIONS

1. Chill the chicken meat for 6 to 12 hours before canning (either with or without the bones). Soak the meat (either with or without the bones) in a mixture of water and salt (1 tbsp per quart) for one hour, then rinse.

2. Discard any excess fat on the meat before slicing it into one-inch chunks.

3. Boil the meat chunks until almost done. Meanwhile, fill your clean and hot Mason jars with salt (1 tsp per quart). Add the boiled meat and hot liquid, making sure to leave a quarter of an inch of headspace.

4. If choosing to raw pack chicken, place in clean and hot Mason jars, packing them in loosely and leaving 1¼-inch of headspace. For each quart, add one tsp salt (no liquids).

5. Get rid of air bubbles before adjusting the lids on the jars, process in the pressure canner for 1 hour and 15 minutes (for pint jars) or 1 hour and 30 minutes (for quart jars).

6. Serve warm.

NUTRITION

Calories: 104 Kcal	Fat: 4.1 g	Protein: 1.3 g
Cholesterol: 0 mg	Carbohydrates: 16.3 g	Sugar: 0 g

GROUND TURKEY TACO SALAD

🥣 6 | **Prep Time : 20 Mins** | **Cook Time : 0 Mins**

INGREDIENTS

- ½ lb ground turkey
- 1 tbsp olive oil
- 1 tsp chili powder
- ½ tsp cumin
- ¼ tsp garlic powder
- ¼ tsp salt
- ½ cup salsa
- 2 tbsp mashed avocado
- ½ tsp lemon juice
- 1 cup halved cherry tomatoes
- 3 cups chopped romaine lettuce
- ½ cup whole grain tortilla chips
- ½ cup shredded cheddar cheese, shredded

DIRECTIONS

1. Heat the olive oil in a sizable skillet over medium-high heat. Fry the ground turkey together with chili powder, cumin, garlic powder, and salt until it is completely cooked.

2. Put on a clean bowl and let it cool completely.

3. In a mini bowl, mix the mashed avocado with the lemon juice.

4. Spoon the salsa equally into 6 pint-sized canning jars, followed by the mashed avocado.

5. Next, layer the jars with cooled turkey, tomatoes, and lettuce, and top it off with the broken tortilla chips and shredded cheese.

NUTRITION

Calories: 278 Kcal Fat: 17 g Protein: 23 g

Cholesterol: 0 mg Carbohydrates: 11 g Sugar: 0 g

59.

CANNED CHICKEN AND GRAVY

🥣 5 | Prep Time : 10 Mins | Cook Time : 35 Mins

INGREDIENTS

·1 cup chopped onion

·1 cup chopped celery

·1 cup diced potatoes

·2 lb boneless chicken breasts

·2 tsp salt

·2 tsp poultry seasoning

·4 tbsp white wine

·Enough chicken stock to fill the jars

DIRECTIONS

1.   Sterilize the jars in a pressure canner as indicated in the general guidelines of this book. Allow the jars to cool.

2.   Place all ingredients in a saucepan and allow to simmer for 10 minutes over medium-high heat.

3.   Put the chicken and vegetables into the jars. Pour over enough broth to cover the chicken. Leave a ½ inch of headspace.

4.   Remove the air bubbles and close the lid.

5.   Place the jars in the pressure canner. Place in a pressure canner and process for 25 minutes.

NUTRITION

Calories: 562 kcal	Protein: 77.7 g	Fat: 22.2 g
Cholesterol: 0 mg	Sugar: 0 g	Carbohydrates: 7.1 g

CHICKEN AND MUSHROOM CACCIATORE

🥣 4 | ✂️ **Prep Time : 20 Mins** | 🕐 **Cook Time : 0 Mins**

INGREDIENTS

- 4 lb chopped chicken breasts and thighs
- 2 cups chopped mixed bell peppers
- 3 quartered onions
- 2 cups sliced mushrooms
- ¼ tsp salt
- 8 smashed garlic cloves
- 1 bottle red wine
- 4 cups diced tomatoes with juice
- 2 tbsp dried oregano
- 2 tbsp dried basil
- 2 tbsp dried thyme
- ¼ tsp black pepper

DIRECTIONS

1. Layer chicken, peppers, onions, mushrooms, and garlic in quart jars. Season with salt and pepper.
2. Boil the wine, tomatoes, and herbs in a stock pot. Season with salt and pepper.
3. Put the hot liquid over the layered ingredients in your jars.
4. Lid the jars and process them in your pressure canner for 90 minutes at 11 PSI, adjusting for altitude.

NUTRITION

Calories: 223.6 Kcal	Fat: 15.6 g	Protein: 9.0 g
Cholesterol: 0 mg	Carbohydrates: 13.1 g	Sugar: 0 g

61.

TURKEY AND GREEN BEANS

🍲 4   **Prep Time : 20 Mins**   **Cook Time : 0 Mins**

INGREDIENTS

- 4 cups shredded cooked turkey
- 2 cups cut green beans
- 1½ cup chopped carrots
- 1 cup sliced onion
- 2 cups chicken or turkey broth

DIRECTIONS

1. In a small stockpot, combine the turkey, green beans, carrots, onion, and broth. Bring to a boil over medium-high heat.
2. Leave to cook for 5 minutes, then remove from the fire.
3. Arrange the hot jars on a cutting board.
4. Ladle the hot mixture using a funnel into the jars, leaving some headspace. Remove any air bubbles and add further mixture if necessary.
5. Rinse the rim of each jar with a warm cloth dipped in white vinegar.
6. Add 3 quarts of water and add 2 tbsp distilled white vinegar to the pressure canner.
7. Put the jars in the pressure canner, lock the pressure canner lid, and bring to a boil over high heat for 10 minutes.
8. Process for 90 minutes (quarts) and 75 minutes (pints).
9. Let the pressure in the canner reach zero, then remove the jars after 10 minutes.

NUTRITION

Calories: 202.2 Kcal   Carbohydrates: 9.6 g   Protein: 20.3 g

Cholesterol: 0 mg   Fat: 8.6 g   Sugar: 0 g

CANNED TURKEY

🥣 5   ✂ Prep Time : 10 Mins   Cook Time : 35 Mins

INGREDIENTS

- ·2 lb turkey breasts, sliced into bite-sized pieces
- ·½ tsp canning salt per pint of water
- 2 cups Water

DIRECTIONS

1. Sterilize the jars in a pressure canner as indicated in the general guidelines of this book. Allow the jars to cool.

2. Place the turkey breasts in boiling water and allow to simmer for 10 minutes. Strain the cooked turkey and pack them in the sterilized jars.

3. In a pan, bring water to a boil and add ½ tsp canning salt per pint of water. Stir to dissolve the salt.

4. Pour pickling solution into the jar to cover the turkey. Leave an inch of headspace.

5. Remove the air bubbles and close the lid.

6. Place the jars in the pressure canner. Place in a pressure canner and process for 25 minutes.

NUTRITION

Calories: 285 Kcal	Protein: 39.7 g	Fat: 12.7 g
Cholesterol: 0 mg	Sugar: 0 g	Carbohydrates: 0 g

63.

CANNED ROSEMARY CHICKEN

🍲 10   **Prep Time : 20 Mins**   **Cook Time : 0 Mins**

INGREDIENTS

· 20 sprigs of rosemary

· 10 lb boneless chicken breast

· ¼ cup salt

DIRECTIONS

1. Add a sprig of rosemary to each sterilized jar.

2. Slice the chicken breasts into large chunks and pack them in the jars leaving a 1.5-inch headspace.

3. Add a sprig of rosemary at the top then add a tbsp salt in each jar.

4. Rinse the rims of the jar with a clean damp towel, and then place the lids and the rings. Transfer the jars to the pressure canner and process them at 10 lb pressure for 75 minutes.

5. Wait for the pressure canner to depressurize to zero before removing the jars using cooking tongs.

6. Transfer the jars to a cooling rack for 24 hours to seal then store them in a cool dry place.

NUTRITION

Calories: 182.6 Kcal	Fat: 7.8 g	Protein: 18.8 g
Cholesterol: 0 mg	Carbohydrates: 1.0 g	Sugar: 0 g

CANNED TURKEY PIECES

🥣 5   Prep Time : 20 Mins   🕐 Cook Time : 0 Mins

INGREDIENTS

- ·5 lb turkey
- ·1 pot Boiling water

DIRECTIONS

1. Use a method of your choice to cook the turkey meat until it is cooked.

2. Pack the turkey pieces in the sterilized jars, then add water or stock leaving 1-inch headspace.

3. Remove the air bubbles and place them. Wipe the rims with a damp cloth.

4. Put the lids and the rings on the jars. Transfer the jars to the pressure canner and process them at 10 lb pressure for 65 minutes if the turkey had bones and for 75 minutes if without bones.

5. Wait for the pressure canner to depressurize to zero before removing the jars.

6. Place the jars on a cooling rack for 24 hours then store them in a cool dry place.

NUTRITION

Calories: 262 Kcal	Fat: 10.1 g	Protein: 25 g
Cholesterol: 0 mg	Carbohydrates: 40 g	Sugar: 0 g

65.

BARBEQUE-SAUCED CHICKEN

🥣 6   **Prep Time : 20 Mins**   **Cook Time : 0 Mins**

INGREDIENTS

- 2 lb chopped chicken
- 1 crushed garlic clove
- cup light brown sugar
- cup soy sauce
- ½ cup water
- 1 tbsp cider vinegar
- ¼ cup apple juice
- 1 tsp crushed red pepper
- 2 tbsp ketchup
- 2 tbsp oil

DIRECTIONS

1. Sterilize the jars.
2. Add all the ingredients in a pot except the oil and chicken, and bring them to a boil.
3. Melt the oil in a pan and stir-fry the chicken in it until lightly browned.
4. Ladle the chicken and the liquid immediately into the sterilized jars, leaving 1 inch of headspace.
5. Remove any air bubbles and clean the rims.
6. Cover the jars with the lid and apply the bands, ensuring that it is tightened.
7. Process the jars for 75 minutes at 1000 feet in a pressure canner.
8. Remove, let it cool, and then label the jars.

NUTRITION

Calories: 212.9 kcal   Fat: 1.9 g   Protein: 35.7 g

Cholesterol: 0 mg   Carbohydrates: 13.5 g   Sugar: 3.97 g

PINEAPPLE CHICKEN

6   **Prep Time : 20 Mins**   **Cook Time : 0 Mins**

INGREDIENTS

- 3 cups pineapple juice
- ¾ cup brown sugar
- 1¼ cup apple cider vinegar
- 6 tbsp soy sauce
- 4 tbsp tomato paste
- 1 tsp ground ginger
- 4 minced garlic cloves
- 5 lb chopped boneless and skinless chicken
- 2 diced onions
- 3 diced bell peppers
- 1 diced pineapple
- Crushed chili pepper, to taste

DIRECTIONS

1. In a sizable saucepan, bring to a boil pineapple juice, sugar, vinegar, soy sauce, tomato paste, ginger, and garlic, stirring frequently.
2. Boil for the sugar to dissolve and until the mixture is smooth.
3. In your jars, layer chicken, onions, peppers, and pineapple. If you're using crushed chilis, add them now.
4. Put the sauce over the contents of the jars.
5. Wipe the rims of the jars, put the lids on, and process in a pressure canner at 11 PSI for 90 minutes, adjusting for altitude.

NUTRITION

Calories: 391 Kcal	Fat: 3.5 g	Protein: 19.5 g
Cholesterol: 0 mg	Carbohydrates: 32.6 g	Sugar: 340.44 g

67.

BLACK-EYED PEAS

 7   **Prep Time : 10 Mins**   **Cook Time : 30 Mins**

INGREDIENTS

- 1½ lb dried black-eyed peas, soaked overnight and drained
- 6 tbsp onions, chopped
- 4 tsp dried thyme
- 1½ tsp kosher salt
- 30 peppercorns

DIRECTIONS

1. In a Dutch oven, add black-eyed peas and enough water to cover over high heat and cook until boiling. Adjust the heat to low and cook for about 30 minutes.
2. Drain the black-eyed peas, reserving cooking liquid. In 3 (1-pint) hot sterilized jars, divide the black-eyed peas, onion, thyme, salt, and peppercorn.
3. Fill each jar with hot cooking liquid, leaving a 1-inch space from the top. Run your knife around the insides of each jar to remove any air bubbles.
4. Wipe any trace of food off the rims of jars with a clean, moist kitchen towel. Close each jar with a lid and screw on the ring.
5. Carefully place the jars in the pressure canner and process at 10 lb pressure for about 75 minutes.
6. Remove the jars from the pressure canner and place them onto a wood surface several inches apart to cool completely.
7. After cooling with your finger, press the top of each jar's lid to ensure that the seal is tight. Store these canning jars in a cool, dark place.

NUTRITION

Calories: 196 Kcal	Carbohydrates: 34 g
Fat: 0.8 g	Protein: 13.6 g

RED LENTILS

🥣 8   **Prep Time : 10 Mins**   🕐 **Cook Time : 10 Mins**

INGREDIENTS

·2 cups red lentils, rinsed

·4 cups chicken broth

·2 small brown onions, chopped finely

DIRECTIONS

1. In a Dutch oven, add lentils, onion, and broth over high heat and cook until boiling. Now set the heat to low and cook for about 5 minutes.

2. In 4 (1-pint) hot sterilized jars, divide the lentils. Fill each jar with hot cooking liquid, leaving a 1-inch space from the top.

3. Run your knife around the insides of each jar to remove any air bubbles. Wipe any trace of food off the rims of jars with a clean, moist kitchen towel.

4. Close each jar with a lid and screw on the ring. Carefully place the jars in the pressure canner and process at 10 lb pressure for about 75 minutes.

5. Remove the jars from the pressure canner and place them onto a wood surface several inches apart to cool completely.

6. After cooling with your finger, press the top of each jar's lid to ensure that the seal is tight. Store these canning jars in a cool, dark place.

NUTRITION

Calories: 196 Kcal	Carbohydrates: 30.9 g
Fat: 1.2 g	Protein: 15 g

69.

CANNED CORN

🥣 8   Prep Time : 15 Mins   Cook Time : 55 Mins

INGREDIENTS

- 12 ears corn
- 1½ tsp salt

DIRECTIONS

1. Husk corn and remove silk. Wash corn cobs and cut corn from the cob. In 3 (1-pint) hot sterilized jars, divide the corn and salt.

2. Fill each jar with hot water, leaving a 1-inch space from the top. Run your knife around the insides of each jar to remove any air bubbles.

3. Wipe any trace of food off the rims of jars with a clean, moist kitchen towel. Close each jar with a lid and screw on the ring.

4. Carefully place the jars in the pressure canner and process at 10 lb pressure for about 55 minutes.

5. Remove the jars from the pressure canner and place them onto a wood surface several inches apart to cool completely.

6. After cooling with your finger, press the top of each jar's lid to ensure that the seal is tight. Store these canning jars in a cool, dark place.

NUTRITION

Calories: 132 Kcal   Carbohydrates: 29 g

Fat: 1.9 g   Protein: 5 g

SWEET & SOUR BEANS

🥣 8   🍴 Prep Time : 15 Mins   🕐 Cook Time : 30 Mins

INGREDIENTS

- 1 lb navy beans
- ½ cup leeks, chopped
- 2 cups water
- 2 cups ketchup
- 1 cup maple syrup
- ½ cup molasses
- 2 tbsp brown sugar
- 1½ tsp mustard powder
- Salt and ground black pepper, as needed
- ½ cup white vinegar

DIRECTIONS

1. In a Dutch oven, add beans and enough water to cover over high heat and cook until boiling. Remove the pan of beans from heat and set aside, covering for about 30 to 45 minutes.
2. Drain the beans and then add enough fresh water to cover them. Add the leeks and cook for about 15 to 20 minutes. Remove the pan of beans from the heat and drain the water.
3. In a nonreactive saucepan, add 2 cups of water and the remaining ingredients (except for vinegar) and bring to a gentle boil, stirring continuously.
4. Remove the pan of the cooking mixture from the heat and stir in vinegar. In 4 (1-pint) hot sterilized jars, divide the beans. Fill each jar with hot vinegar mixture, leaving a 1-inch space from the top.

5. Run your knife around the insides of each jar to remove any air bubbles. Wipe any trace of food off the rims of jars with a clean, moist kitchen towel.

6. Close each jar with a lid and screw on the ring. Carefully place the jars in the pressure canner and process at 10 lb pressure for about 75 minutes.

7. Remove the jars from the pressure canner and place them onto a wood surface several inches apart to cool completely.

8. After cooling with your finger, press the top of each jar's lid to ensure that the seal is tight. Store these canning jars in a cool, dark place.

NUTRITION

Calories: 389 Kcal	Carbohydrates: 85.1 g
Fat: 1.1 g	Protein: 13.7 g

71.

BEEF STEW

 7   Prep Time : 5 Mins   Cook Time : 30 Mins

INGREDIENTS

- 4 to 5 lb beef stew meat1 ½-inch cubes
- 1 tbsp vegetable oil
- 12 cups potatoes, peeled and cubed
- 8 cups carrots, sliced
- 3 cups celery, chopped
- 3 cups onion, chopped
- 1 ½ tbsp salt
- 1 tbsp thyme
- ½ tbsp pepper
- Water, to cover

DIRECTIONS

1. Brown meat in a large saucepot, in oil.
2. Add vegetables and all the seasonings, then cover with water. Boil the stew and remove it from the heat.
3. Scoop the hot stew into hot quart jars. Leave a 1-inch headspace.
4. If needed, remove air bubbles by adjusting the headspace. Wipe the rims of the jars using a paper towel, dampened clean.
5. Now apply the 2-piece metal caps.
6. Process the quart jars in a pressure canner for about 90 minutes at 11 lb pressure if using a dial-gauge canner, or at 10 lb pressure if using a weighted-gauge canner.

NUTRITION

Calories: 877 Kcal	Fat: 22.6 g	Protein: 104.6 g
Cholesterol: 0 mg	Carbohydrates: 59.2 g	Sugar: 11.8 g

CANNED HEARTY CHILI STEW

🥣 6   ✂ **Prep Time : 10 Mins**   🕐 **Cook Time : 60 Mins**

INGREDIENTS

- 4 lb beef chunk, boneless, fat removed, and ½-inch cubes
- ¼ cup vegetable oil
- 3 cups onion, diced
- 2 minced garlic cloves
- 5 tbsp chili powder
- 2 tbsp cumin seed
- 2 tbsp salt
- 1 tbsp oregano
- ½ tbsp pepper
- ½ tbsp coriander
- ½ tbsp red pepper, crushed
- 6 cups canned tomatoes, diced and not drained

DIRECTIONS

1. Brown the meat cubes in hot oil lightly, then add garlic and onions. Cook until soft and not brown.

2. Add all the remaining spices and cook for about 5 minutes.

3. Add tomatoes and stir, then bring to a boil on high.

4. Reduce to medium-low heat and simmer for about 45 to 60 minutes. Stir occasionally.

5. Scoop hot chili stew into hot pint jars. Leave a 1-inch headspace.

6. If needed, remove the air bubbles, adjusting the headspace. Wipe the rims of the jars using a paper towel, dampened clean.

7. Now apply the 2-piece metal caps.

8. Process the pint jars in a pressure canner for about 90 minutes at 11 lb pressure if using a dial-gauge canner, or at 10 lb pressure if using a weighted-gauge canner.

NUTRITION

Calories: 733 Kcal	Fat: 30 g	Protein: 95.6 g	Fiber: 6.4 g
Cholesterol: 0 mg	Carbohydrates: 18.6 g	Sugar: 8.2 g	

73.

CHICKEN NOODLE SOUP

 4   **Prep Time : 10 Mins**   **Cook Time : 25 Mins**

INGREDIENTS

- ¼ cup red lentils
- 1 bay leaf
- 1 cup egg noodles
- tsp celery seed
- tsp garlic powder
- ½ tsp dill seed
- 1 ½ tbsp chicken bouillon granules
- 2 tbsp dehydrated sliced onion
- 8 cups water

DIRECTIONS

1. Add all ingredients except water into the glass jar. Seal the jar with the lid tightly and shake well.
2. To cook, add water and jar content to the saucepan and bring to a boil.
3. Reduce heat and simmer for 25 minutes.
4. Serve and enjoy.

NUTRITION

Calories: 108 Kcal	Fat: 1.1 g	Carbohydrates: 19.6 g
Cholesterol: 0 mg	Protein: 5.2 g	Sugar: 0 g

BUTTER SQUASH SOUP

🥣 **10-12 Pints** 🍴 **Prep Time : 15 Mins** 🕐 **Cook Time : 75 Mins**

INGREDIENTS

·1 large/2 small butternut squashes, peeled, cubed

·2 apples, peeled and sliced

·2 red onions, peeled and sliced

·5 carrots, medium-sized, peeled and sliced

·2 sweet potatoes, peeled, cubed

·3 tsp salt, optional

DIRECTIONS

1.   In hot jars, layer squash, apple, onions, and carrots equally in all jars. Leave headspace of 1-inch. Add ¼ tsp in each jar, if desired.

2.   Pour boiling water over vegetables and leave a headspace of 1-inch. Remove air bubbles. Clean the rim of the glass jar. Place the lid and apply a band around it. Adjust to ensure that the lid is tight.

3.   In a pressure canner, place jars on racks with simmering water (2-inches, 90°C/180°F).

4.   Place lid on canner, and adjust medium–high heat. Vent steam for 10 minutes at 10/11 lb (psi for weighted gauge/dial-gauge canner). Process pint jars for 75 minutes or quarts for 90 minutes.

5.   Turn off the canner, and remove the lid after 2 minutes when pressure turns zero. Keep the jars in the canner for 10 minutes more.

6.   Remove the jars. Reprocess if the jars are not sealed. Cool and store in the refrigerator.

NUTRITION

Calories: 215 Kcal   Fat: 3 g

Carbohydrates: 35 g   Protein: 15 g

75.

BEEF BONE BROTH

 4 Pints   Prep Time : 15 Mins   Cook Time : 8 H 50 Mins

INGREDIENTS

- 4 lb(2 kg) meaty beef bones
- 2 qt (2 l) water
- 2 tbsp unfiltered apple cider vinegar (5% acidity)
- 2 tsp salt
- 3 garlic cloves, crushed
- 2 bay leaves
- 1 large onion, quartered

DIRECTIONS

1. Preheat the oven to 392°F. In a large roasting pan, place beef bones and bake for 30 minutes. Removes bones.

2. Reduce temperature to 225°F. Place in a Stainless-steel Dutch oven, add bones, pan drippings, water, vinegar, salt, garlic, bay leaves, and onion. Stir well. Cover and bake for 8 hours.

3. Reduce temperature to 194°F and bake for 8 hours more. Remove bones. In a 2L bowl, strain the broth using a fine wire-mesh strainer. Skim fat and discard solids.

4. Add water if the broth doesn't measure 2L. Pour broth into a large Dutch oven and let it simmer.

5. Transfer the broth to hot jars. Leave headspace of 1-inch. Clean the rim of the glass jar. Place the lid and apply a band around it. Adjust to ensure that the lid is tight.

6. In a pressure canner, place jars on racks with simmering water (2-inches, 90°C/180°F).

7. Place lid on canner, and adjust medium-high heat. Vent steam for 10 minutes at 10/11 lb (psi for weighted gauge/dial-gauge canner).

8. Process pint jars for 20 minutes or quarts for 25 minutes. Turn off the canner and remove the lid after 2 minutes when pressure turns zero. Keep the jars in the canner for 10 minutes more.

9. Remove the jars. Reprocess if the jars are not sealed. Cool and store in the refrigerator.

NUTRITION

Calories: 51 Kcal	Fat: 0 g
Carbohydrates: 3 g	Protein: 8 g

BEEF GARDEN SOUP

9 Jars   **Prep Time : 90 Mins**   **Cook Time : 75 Mins**

INGREDIENTS

- 8 Roma tomatoes
- 5 lb beef chuck roast
- 2 tbsp vegetable oil
- 5 quarts beef broth
- 2 medium potatoes
- 8 carrots, 1-inch diameter
- 3 medium onions
- 2 cups frozen kernel corn
- 4 jalapeño peppers
- 2 tbsp salt
- 4 poblano chili peppers
- 12 garlic cloves
- 1 tbsp ground black pepper
- 1 tbsp chili powder

DIRECTIONS

1. 1 tbsp oil, heated over medium-high heat in a 12-quart saucepan half of the meat cubes should be added now. Cook, constantly stirring, until browned. Place the steak in a mixing basin. Rep with the rest of the meat and 1 tbsp oil.

2. Return all of the steaks to the pot. Pour in the broth. Bring to a boil, then turn off the heat. Cook for 75 minutes, covered, or till meat is tender.

3. To the meat mixture in the saucepan, add tomatoes, sweet potatoes, corn, chili powder, onions, carrots, poblano peppers, garlic, jalapeno peppers, salt, and black pepper. Bring to a boil, then reduce to low heat and cook for 5 minutes, covered.

4. Fill hot, clean 1-quart preserving jars halfway with the meat and veggies. Fill each jar halfway with heated broth, allowing a 1-inch headspace. Adjust lids & screw bands after wiping jar rims.

5. Fill jars & process for 75 minutes in a pressure canner at 10 lb pressure for a weighted-gauge canner or 11 lb pressure for a dial-gauge canner, adjusting for altitude. Allow the pressure to naturally decrease. Remove the canner lid with care and cool the jars in the canner for 10 minutes. Remove the jars from the canner and place them on a wire rack to cool. After 24 hours, check the lids for seal.

6. Place the contents of the jar in a medium saucepan to serve. Bring the water to a quick boil. Cover and cook for 10 minutes (add 1 additional minute for each additional 1000 feet of elevation).

NUTRITION

Calories: 260 Kcal   Protein: 32 g

Carbohydrates: 16 g   Fat: 7 g

77.

CANNED VEGETABLE SOUP

🥣 **6 Quarts**   🍴 **Prep Time : 60 Mins**   🕐 **Cook Time : 80 Mins**

INGREDIENTS

- 4 cups peeled tomatoes
- 4 ½ quarts beef, chicken, or vegetable broth
- 3 cups peeled potatoes
- 4 cups whole-kernel corn
- 2 cups sliced carrots
- 2 cups green beans
- 1 cup chopped onion
- 2 cups sliced celery
- 2 tbsp snipped parsley
- 3 garlic
- 1 tbsp snipped thyme
- 1 tbsp snipped marjoram
- 1 tbsp snipped rosemary
- ½ tsp pepper

DIRECTIONS

1. Mix tomatoes, corn, broth, carrots, potatoes, green beans, onion, garlic, celery, parsley, thyme, marjoram, rosemary, and pepper in an 8-to 10-quart Dutch oven or kettle.

2. Bring to a boil, then turn off the heat. Cover and cook for 5 minutes (vegetables will be crisp).

3. Fill hot, clean pint or quart canning jars approximately half-filled with heated veggies. Fill the container halfway with hot liquid, allowing a 1-inch headspace. Air bubbles should be removed, jar rims should be cleaned, and lids should be adjusted.

4. Process full jars in the pressure canner for 120 minutes for quarts or 60 minutes for pints at 10 lb pressure for weighted canners and 11 lb pressure for the dial-gauge canners. Let the pressure naturally decrease.

5. Remove the jars from the canner and place them on racks to cool.

NUTRITION

Calories: 76 Kcal	Protein: 3 g
Carbohydrates: 16 g	Fat: 1 g

ROSEMARY & TOMATO BUTTERNUT BEAN SOUP

6 Quarts | **Prep Time : 90 Mins** | **Cook Time : 30 Mins**

INGREDIENTS

- ⅓ cup olive oil
- 2 medium onions
- 6 garlic cloves
- 6 cups cooked cannellini
- 3 lb butternut squash
- 3 cups grape tomatoes
- 3 ½ quarts chicken broth
- 1 tbsp rosemary
- 1 ½ tsp salt
- ½ tsp black pepper

DIRECTIONS

1. Heat the oil in an 8-to 10-quart saucepan over medium-high heat. Cook, often stirring, for 7 to 8 minutes, or until golden. Cook for 1 minute, stirring constantly. Combine the beans, tomatoes, squash, rosemary, broth, salt, and pepper in a large mixing bowl. Bring to a boil, then turn off the heat. Cover & cook for 5 minutes.

2. Fill heated quart canning jars halfway with soup, providing a 1-inch headspace. Replace lids as well as screw bands after wiping jar rims.

3. Adjust for altitude and process full jars in a pressure canner for 75 minutes at 10 lb pressure for only a weighted-gauge canner or 11 lb pressure for just a dial-gauge canner. Allow the pressure to naturally decrease. Remove the canner lid with care and cool the jars in the canner for 10 minutes. Remove the jars from the canner and place them on a wire rack to cool. After 24 hours, check the lids for seal.

4. Place the ingredients in a jar inside a small saucepan to serve. Bring the water to a quick boil. Cover and cook for 10 minutes.

NUTRITION

Calories: 163 Kcal | Protein: 8 g
Carbohydrates: 25 g | Fat: 5 g

79.

CHICKEN MEXICAN SOUP CANNING

🥣 7 Quarts   Prep Time : 90 Mins   Cook Time : 75 Mins

INGREDIENTS

- 3 large boneless chicken breasts
- 1 ½ cup carrots
- 2 cups celery
- 1 large onion chopped,
- 2 (14 ½ oz) cans of Rotel tomatoes
- 2 (15 oz) cans of kidney beans
- 4 cups diced tomatoes
- 6 cups water
- 6 cups chicken broth
- 3 cups corn
- 1 tsp ground cumin
- 1 tbsp canning salt
- 3 garlic cloves
- 3 chicken bouillon cubes

DIRECTIONS

1. Cook the chicken in a covered pot until it is done. You may shred the chicken or chop it into 1-inch cubes after it has cooled. Set aside.

2. Set up a pressure canner. In a saucepan of simmering water, heat the jars and lids until they are ready to use. (Do not bring to a boil.)

3. Except for the chicken, combine all the ingredients in a big saucepan. Bring to a boil, then reduce to low heat and cook for 3 minutes. Add the chicken and cook for 5 minutes on low heat.

4. Remove air bubbles and clean jar rims after ladling hot soup into the hot jars, leaving 1-inch headspace. Place the heated lid in the middle of the jar. Apply the band and tighten it with your fingers. In a pressure canner, place the jars.

5. Process quarts for 90 minutes at 11 lb pressure or pints for 75 minutes (adjust for the altitude if needed).

6. Remove the jars and set them aside to cool. After 24 hours, check the lids for seal. When the center of the lid is squeezed, it should not bend up and down.

NUTRITION

Calories: 371 Kcal   Protein: 28.5 g

Carbohydrates: 46.4 g   Fat: 9.4 g

TURKEY SOUP

🥣 10   🍴 **Prep Time : 10 Mins**   🕐 **Cook Time : 120 Mins**

INGREDIENTS

·3 ½ cups diced turkey

·16 cups chicken stock

·1 ½ cup sliced carrots

·1 cup onion

·1 ½ cup diced celery

·Chicken bouillon

·Salt & pepper to taste

DIRECTIONS

1. In a stockpot, combine all of the ingredients and bring them to a boil. Prepare the jars as well as the lids. Fill heated jars halfway with soup, allowing 1" headspace. Make sure the jars are empty of air bubbles.

2. Put the lids and rings on after wiping the rims. Tighten your finger.

3. Prepare the pressure canner according to the manufacturer's instructions. Place jars in a canner and process for 75 minutes at 11 lb for pints and 90 minutes for quarts in a dial gauge canner or 10 lb in a weighted gauge canner. Maintain constant pressure the entire time.

4. Before opening the canner, make sure the pressure has returned to zero.

NUTRITION

Calories: 260 Kcal	Protein: 29 g
Carbohydrates: 25 g	Fat: 4.8 g

81.

TURKEY & VEGETABLE SOUP

🥣 6 Quarts ✕ Prep Time : 60 Mins 🕐 Cook Time : 75 Mins

INGREDIENTS

- 16 cups turkey stock
- 3 cups diced turkey
- 1-½ cup diced celery
- 1-½ cup sliced carrots
- 1 cup diced onion
- Salt, optional
- Pepper, optional

DIRECTIONS

1. In a large stockpot, combine the turkey, celery, turkey stock, carrots, & onion. Bring the liquid to a boil. Reduce heat to low and cook for 30 minutes. If desired, season with salt & pepper to taste.

2. Ladle turkey and vegetables into each jar until about ½ to ¾ filled - you'll need to even out and check the jars to make sure the turkey and veggies are evenly distributed. Finish by ladling hot soup stock into the jars, allowing 1-inch headspace. Air bubbles should be removed. Vinegar should be used to clean the rims. Place the heated lid in the middle of the jar. Adjust the band until it is fingertip tight.

3. Adjust for altitude and process full jars in a Pressure Canner at 11 lb pressure for 1 hour & 15 minutes for pints and 1 hour & 30 minutes for quarts. Remove the jars and set them aside to cool. After 24 hours, check the lids for seal. When the center of the lid is squeezed, it should not bend up and down.

4. Wash the jars and keep them in a cold, dark area without the rings.

NUTRITION

Calories: 569 Kcal	Protein: 15 g
Carbohydrates: 112 g	Fat: 8 g

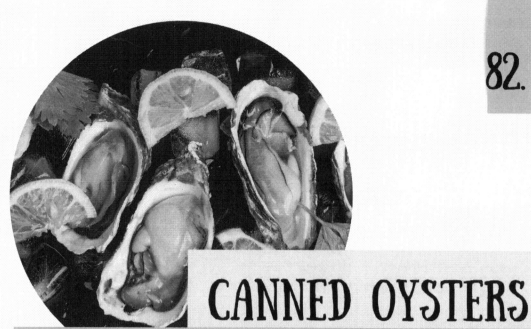

CANNED OYSTERS

🥣 **6 Pints** ✂️ **Prep Time : 15 Mins** 🕐 **Cook Time : 70 Mins**

INGREDIENTS

- ·5 lb oysters
- ·Salt to taste
- 1 pot Water

DIRECTIONS

1. Wash the oysters in clean water, then heat them in an oven at 400°F for 7 minutes to open. Cool them in ice-cold water. Remove the meat, placing it in water containing salt.

2. Drain the meat and pack it in the jars, leaving 1-inch headspace. Add ½ tbsp salt in each half-pint jar and add water, maintaining the headspace.

3. Wipe the jar rims, then place the lids and the rings. Can for 75 minutes at 10 lb. Wait for the pressure canner to depressurize to zero before removing the jars from the canner.

4. Place the jars on a cooling rack undisturbed, then store them in a cool dry place.

NUTRITION

Calories: 68 Kcal	Carbohydrates: 0 g
Fat: 3 g	Protein: 7 g

83.

CANNED TROUT

 6 Pints   **Prep Time : 15 Mins**   **Cook Time : 105 Mins**

INGREDIENTS

- 6 whole trout
- 6 tbsp lemon juice (1 tbsp per jar)
- 6 rosemary springs
- ½ tsp salt

DIRECTIONS

1. Place 1 rosemary spring in the trout's cavity. Salt the inside with ½ tsp salt and close it. Pack jars with trout. Add 1 tbsp lemon juice to each jar.

2. Process for 1 hour and 45 minutes at 10 lb pressure for the weighted gauge of the pressure canner or 11 lb if the pressure canner has a dial gauge.

3. Remove the jars and let them cool until at room temperature.

NUTRITION

Calories: 110 Kcal   Carbohydrates: 0 g

Fat: 6.1 g   Protein: 13.9 g

MINCED CLAMS

 8 Pints | **Prep Time : 15 Mins** | 🕐 **Cook Time : 65 Mins**

INGREDIENTS

- ·2 lb live clams
- ·1 tsp salt in each jar
- ·1 pot Boiling water
- ·2 tbsp lemon juice or ½ tsp citric acid.

DIRECTIONS

1. Scrub the clamshells thoroughly before rinsing and steaming for 5 minutes. Open to remove the meat; reserve the juices.

2. Wash the collected clam meat with a mixture of water and salt (1 tsp per quart). Rinse and place in a pot filled with boiling water (1 gallon) and lemon juice (2 tbsp) or citric acid (½ tsp).

3. Heat until boiling, and then boil for 2 minutes. Drain before placing in clean and hot Mason jars.

4. Pack the clam meat loosely before adding in the hot clam juice, filling the jars up to one inch from the top.

5. After getting rid of air bubbles, adjust the jar lids. Process in the pressure canner for 1 hour (for pint jars) or 1 hour and 10 minutes (for quart jars).

NUTRITION

Calories: 104 Kcal	Carbohydrates: 16.3 g
Fat: 4.1 g	Protein: 1.3 g

85.

CANNED MACKEREL

🍜 3 Pints   Prep Time : 15 Mins   Cook Time : 100 Mins

INGREDIENTS

- 2 lb mackerel fish
- 1 tbsp Vinegar
- Salt to taste

DIRECTIONS

1. Rinse the fish in cold water mixed with vinegar (2 tbsp for each quart).Discard the scales, head, fins, and tail of the fish, then wash thoroughly to remove all blood.

2. Split the fish into lengthwise halves before cutting into 3 ½-inch long pieces. Put in clean and hot Mason jars, each filled with 1 tsp salt but without adding any liquid.

3. Adjust the lids on the jars before placing them in the pressure canner. Process for 1 hour and 40 minutes.

NUTRITION

Calories: 104 Kcal   Carbohydrates: 16.3 g

Fat: 4.1 g   Protein: 1.3 g

CANNED SHRIMP

🍜 10 | ✂ Prep Time : 20 Mins | 🕐 Cook Time : 45 Mins

INGREDIENTS

- 10 lb shrimp
- ¼ cup salt
- 1 cup vinegar

DIRECTIONS

1. Remove the heads immediately, then chill until ready to preserve them.
2. Wash the shrimp and drain them well.
3. Add a gallon of water to a pot, then add salt and vinegar. Bring to a boil, then cook shrimp for 10 minutes.
4. Remove the shrimp from the cooking liquid with a slotted spoon, then rinse in cold water and drain. Peel the shrimp while packing them in the sterilized jars.
5. Add a gallon of water with 3 tbsp salt and bring it to a boil. Add the brine to the jars and remove the air bubbles. Add more brine if necessary.
6. Wipe the jar rims with a cloth damped in vinegar. Place the lids and the rings.
7. Process at 10 lb pressure for 45 minutes.
8. Wait for the pressure canner to depressurize to zero before removing the jars.
9. Place the jars on an undisturbed cooling rack, then store them in a cool, dry place.

NUTRITION

Calories: 100 Kcal	Fat: 2 g	Protein: 15 g
Cholesterol: 0 mg	Carbohydrates: 1 g	Sugar: 0 g

87.

CANNED SALMON

 6   **Prep Time : 20 Mins**   **Cook Time : 100 Mins**

INGREDIENTS

- ·5 lb salmon
- ·Salt to taste

DIRECTIONS

1. Eviscerate the salmon immediately after catching it, then clean it thoroughly with clean water.

2. Chill it until you are ready to pressure, can it. Remove the tail, the head, and the fins. Split the fish lengthwise, then cut it into small pieces that perfectly fit into your jars.

3. Pack the fish in sterilized jars, leaving 1-inch headspace. Add a tbsp salt in each jar if you desire.

4. Rinse the jar rims with a damp paper towel, then place the lids and the rings on the jar.

5. Pressure-can the jars in the pressure canner at 11 lb pressure for 100 minutes.

6. Wait for the pressure canner to depressurize to zero before removing the jars.

7. Transfer the jars to a cooling rack for 24 hours, then store them in a cool, dry place.

NUTRITION

Calories: 121 Kcal	Fat: 5.4 g	Protein: 17 g
Cholesterol: 0 mg	Carbohydrates: 0 g	Sugar: 0 g

CHAPTER 6: FRUITS AND VEGETABLES

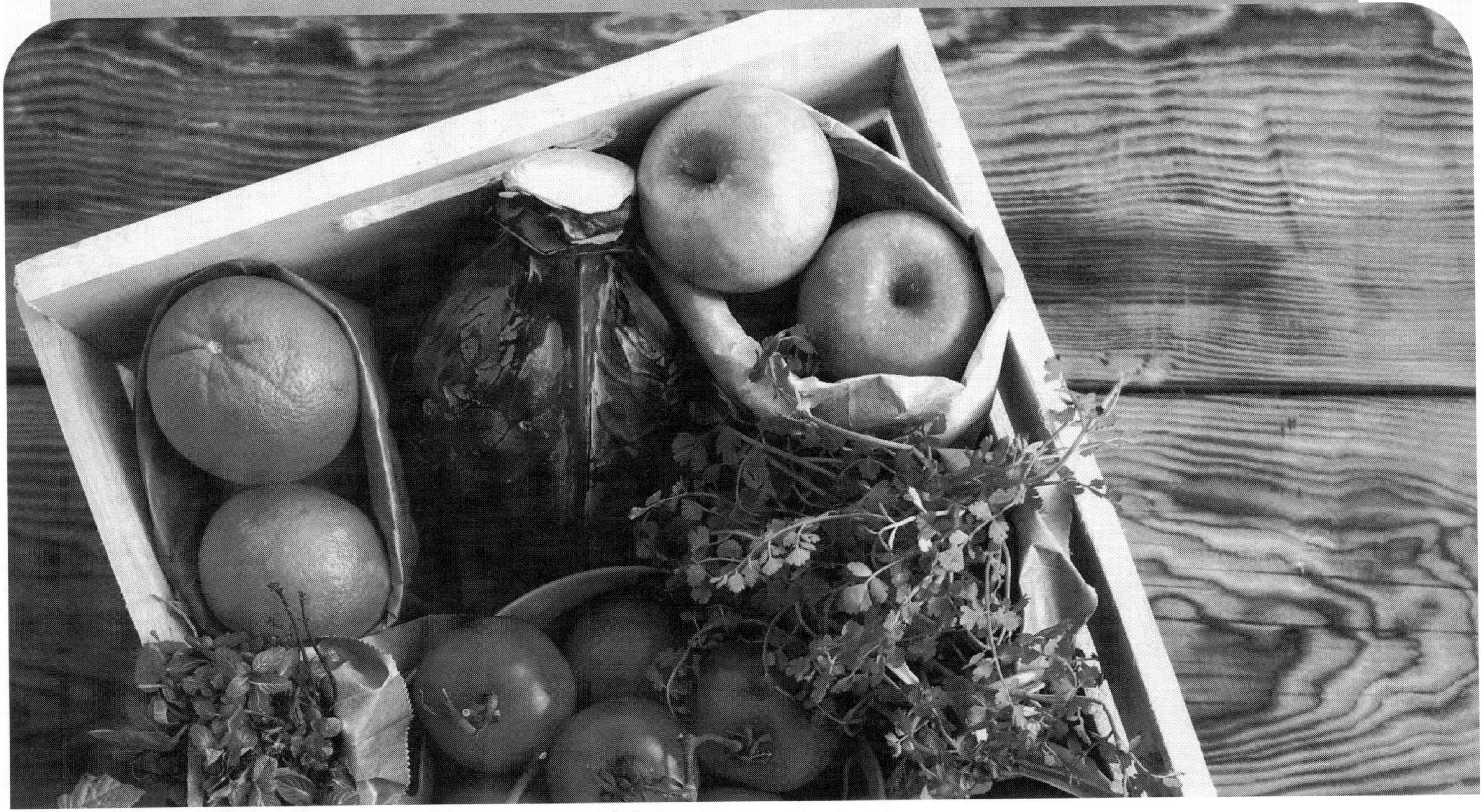

88.

CANNED APRICOTS

 8   **Prep Time : 10 Mins**   **Cook Time : 20 Mins**

INGREDIENTS

- 2 lb apricots, washed, cut in half, and removed the stone
- 4 cups water
- 2 cups sugar

DIRECTIONS

1. Add water and sugar to a pot and cook over medium heat until the sugar is melted.
2. Add apricots into the jars.
3. Pour sugar syrup over apricots.
4. Cover jars with lids.
5. Place jars in a large pot and cover them with water. Bring to a boil and simmer for 30 minutes.
6. Turn off the heat and let the jars cool completely.
7. Check the seals of jars. Label and store.

NUTRITION

Calories: 240 Kcal	Fat: 1 g	Sugar: 60 g
Cholesterol: 0 mg	Carbohydrates: 62 g	Protein: 1.5 g

CANNED PINEAPPLE

 24   **Prep Time : 10 Mins**   **Cook Time : 60 Mins**

INGREDIENTS

- 6 large pineapples, peeled, cored & cut into chunks
- 5 cups water
- 1 cup sugar

DIRECTIONS

1. Add sugar and water into the pot and bring to a boil; stir constantly until sugar is dissolved. Reduce heat to low.
2. Add pineapple chunks and cook for 10 minutes.
3. Pack pineapple chunks into the clean jars. Leave ½-inch headspace.
4. Pour hot sugar syrup over pineapple chunks. Leave ½-inch headspace. Remove air bubbles.
5. Seal jars with lids and process in a boiling water bath for 10 minutes.
6. Remove jars from the water bath and let them cool completely.
7. Check the seals of jars. Label and store.

NUTRITION

Calories: 72 Kcal	Fat: 0.1 g	Sugar: 16.5 g
Cholesterol: 0 mg	Carbohydrates: 19.2 g	Protein: 0.4 g

90.

CANNED PEARS

 7　　 **Prep Time : 10 Mins**　　 **Cook Time : 25 Mins**

INGREDIENTS

- 18 lb pears, peeled and sliced
- 6 cups water
- 1 cup sugar

DIRECTIONS

1. Add water and sugar in a saucepan and bring to a boil over medium heat.
2. Once sugar syrup begins to boil, reduce heat to low.
3. Add pears to the sugar syrup and simmer for 5 minutes.
4. Pack pears into the clean jars. Leave ¼-inch headspace.
5. Pour hot sugar syrup over the pears. Leave ¼-inch headspace. Remove air bubbles.
6. Seal jars with lids and process them in a boiling water bath for 20 minutes.
7. Remove jars from the water bath and let them cool completely.
8. Check the seals of jars. Label and store.

NUTRITION

Calories: 784 Kcal	Fat: 1.7 g	Sugar: 142.5 g
Cholesterol: 0 mg	Carbohydrates: 206.5 g	Protein: 4.3 g

PICKLED CABBAGE & PEPPER

🥣 **4 Pints**   ✗ **Prep Time : 30 Mins**   🕐 **Cook Time : 10 Mins**

INGREDIENTS

- 2 lb cabbage, cored & shredded
- 5 cups bell peppers, cut into strips
- ¼ cup pickling salt
- 1 cup sugar
- 1 ½ cup white wine vinegar
- ½ tsp hot pepper flakes
- 4 tsp mustard seeds
- 6 garlic cloves

DIRECTIONS

1. Toss the cabbage & peppers with the salt in a big basin or cork. Cover and set aside for 8 to 12 hours in a cool area.

2. Combine the sugar & vinegar in a non-reactive pot. Bring to a boil, then remove from heat.

3. Drain the cabbage well after rinsing it.

4. Combine the mustard seeds, pepper flakes, and garlic in a mixing bowl. Fill pint mason jars halfway with the veggie mixture. (The recipe yields roughly 4 quarts when followed exactly as indicated.) If you need additional jars, it's because you didn't pack them tightly enough, and you'll need an additional vinegar mixture as a consequence.) Over the veggies, pour the vinegar mixture. Hot two-piece caps are used to seal the jars.

5. In a hot water bath, process the jars for 20 minutes. Before consuming the cabbage, keep the cooled jars in a cold, dry, dark area for at least 3 weeks.

NUTRITION

Calories: 304 Kcal	Protein: 5.3 g
Carbohydrates: 73.9 g	Fat: 1.3 g

CANNED CARROTS

🥣 **7 Quarts** ✂️ **Prep Time : 60 Mins** 🕐 **Cook Time : 30 Mins**

INGREDIENTS

- 18 lb carrots
- Salt, optional

DIRECTIONS

1. Peel and cut the carrots before using. Peeling is optional; however, it is strongly encouraged since it enhances the quality of residence carrots significantly.

2. The sliced/diced carrots may be any size, so choose one that will work in upcoming meals for your family.

3. Warm 2 to 3 inches of water at the end of a pressure canner with the bottom trivet in place to prepare a pressure canner.

4. On the stove, bring a saucepan of water to a boil next to the canner.

5. Blanch the carrots in boiling water for 5 minutes before packing them warm into canning jars for a Hot Pack (1-inch headspace). Simply put the carrots into jars without blanching them, leaving a 1 in the headspace. If using a raw pack, make absolutely sure the pressure canner is hot but not hot enough to cause thermal shock. Use a simmering to totally boiling canner for the hot pack.

6. Pour boiling water well over the top of the carrots in jars, leaving 1-inch headspace, regardless of the packing technique. If using, season with salt at a rate of 1 tbsp per quart (or ½ tsp each pint).

7. Fill the pressure canner halfway with jars that have been sealed with two-part canning lids.

8. Place the cover on the canner, bring it to a full boil, and let the steam escape for 10 minutes before inserting the canning weight and letting the pressure buildup.

9. Process for 25 minutes (pints) or 30 minutes (quarts). Below 1000 feet, use 10 lb pressure, but adjust for elevation at higher heights.

10. Allow the canner to come to room temp before opening and emptying the jars after the processing is finished.

11. Check seals and put any jars that aren't sealed in the refrigerator for direct consumption.

12. Jars that have been properly treated and sealed should last 12 to 18 months in the pantry.

NUTRITION

Calories: 279 Kcal	Protein: 5 g	Sugar: 142.5 g
Carbohydrates: 69 g	Fat: 0.2 g	Protein: 4.3 g

CANNED POTATOES

| 🥣 8 Pints | 🍴 Prep Time : 60 Mins | 🕐 Cook Time : 40 Mins |

INGREDIENTS

·Potatoes

·Canning salt

·2 big pots water

DIRECTIONS

1. Bring 2 big pots of water to a rolling boil on the stove. The first is to pre-cook the potatoes, and the second is to use fresh, clean water as the canning liquid in the jars. Important: Do not reuse the potato boiling liquid for packaging.

2. Prepare your potatoes while the water rises to a boil. Peel the potatoes and cut any big ones into 1 to 2-inch chunks.

3. Potatoes with a diameter of fewer than 2 inches may be left whole, but they must still be peeled. To keep the potatoes from browning as you work, place them in a dish of water to keep them immersed.

4. Place the potatoes in the boiling water and pre-cook for 2 minutes (for 1" cubes) or 10 minutes (for entire potatoes around 2" in diameter). After the potatoes have been cooked, strain them and discard the cooking liquid.

5. Fill canning jars halfway with cooked potatoes.

6. 1 tsp salt per quart, covered with clean, boiling water, optional.

7. Apply 2-part canning lids on rims, tightening to just finger tight.

8. Set your pressure canner on the stovetop and fill it halfway with boiling water from a clean boiling water pot. After that, place the hot jars into the pressurized canner using the canning rack that comes with it.

9. Allow 10 minutes for the steam to escape before properly closing the pressure canner with a canning weight.

10. Permit the pressure canner to get up to pressure before starting the timing once the gauge reads the desired pressure. Set the canner to 10 lb pressure & process for 35 minutes (pints) or 40 minutes (quarts) when canning potatoes below 1000 feet elevation (quarts).

NUTRITION

Calories: 259 Kcal	Protein: 8 g
Carbohydrates: 85 g	Fat: 0.2 g

94.

CANNED PEACHES

 8 Pints   **Prep Time : 10 Mins**   **Cook Time : 30 Mins**

INGREDIENTS

- ½ bushel peaches
- 2 ¼ cups granulated sugar
- 5 ¼ cups water

DIRECTIONS

1. In a saucepan, combine the water and some sugar. Bring the solution to a low boil and cook until the sugar is completely dissolved.
2. The peaches will be canned in this syrup; it's important to keep the syrup warm but not so hot that it cooks.
3. Remove the stone from the bleached and skinned peaches by cutting them in half.
4. Refill the jars halfway with peaches that have been peeled and half-filled with heated syrup. You should leave approximately a 12-inch gap at the jar's top.
5. Before utilizing the water bath canning procedure for 15 minutes, secure the lids here on the jars. You can ensure that the heat-resistant germs in your pressure-canned items are destroyed by closely following the processing schedules.

NUTRITION

Calories: 412 Kcal   Protein: 43.8 g

Carbohydrates: 10.4 g   Fat: 20.9 g

BILL'S APPLE BUTTER

8 Pints | **Prep Time : 60 Mins** | **Cook Time : 15 Mins**

INGREDIENTS

- ·15 lb early-season apples
- ·¾ cup cider vinegar
- ·5 cups packed brown sugar
- ·4 cups sugar
- ·2 tbsp the ground cinnamon
- ·1 tsp salt
- ·1 tsp cinnamon extract
- ·½ tsp ground cloves
- ·½ tsp ground allspice
- ·1 cup red-hot candies
- ·1 cup boiling water

DIRECTIONS

1. Bring the apples and vinegar to a boil in a stockpot. Reduce heat to low and cook, uncovered, for 30 to 40 minutes or until vegetables are soft. Remove from the heat and let it cool slightly. In a food processor, mix in batches until smooth. Return everything to the pan.

2. Sugar, brown sugar, salt, cinnamon, extract, cloves, & allspice are combined in a bowl. Red hots should be dissolved in boiling water and then added to the apple mixture.

3. Bring the water to a boil. Reduce heat to low and cook, uncovered, for 2 hours or until the mixture has thickened to a spreadable consistency.

4. Remove the pan from the heat. Carefully spoon the heated mixture into 8 1-pint sterilized jars, allowing ¼-inch headspace. Remove air bubbles and, if required, correct the headspace by adding a heated mixture. Clean the rims. Screw on bands till the fingertip is tight; center lids on jars.

5. Place the jars in a canner filled with simmering water, ensuring they are fully covered. Bring to a boil, then reduce to a simmer for 5 minutes. Remove the jars and set them aside to cool.

NUTRITION

Calories: 92 Kcal | Protein: 0 g

Carbohydrates: 24 g | Fat: 0 g

96.

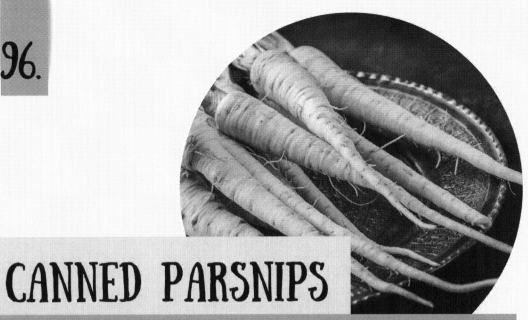

CANNED PARSNIPS

 4 Pints **Prep Time : 15 Mins** **Cook Time : 30 Mins**

INGREDIENTS

- ·½ lb parsnips per pint jar
- ·Salt, optional
- ·Water

DIRECTIONS

1. Wash parsnips thoroughly, then cut them into chunks about 2 inches in size. Then blanch for 4 minutes in boiling water, then dip in an ice bath.

2. Pack parsnips into jars, then pour boiling water into jars, leaving 1-inch headspace. Add salt if preferred.

Process jars for 30 minutes at 10 lb pressure or 11 lb with a dial gauge. Once done, let cool for 12 to 24 hours before removing

NUTRITION

Calories: 75 Kcal   Carbohydrates: 24 g

Protein: 4 g   Fat: 0.5 g

BAEK KIMCHI

🥣 10 ✂️ **Prep Time : 30 Mins** 🕐 **Cook Time : 20 Mins**

INGREDIENTS

·1 head napa cabbage

·3 tbsp salt

·1 cup water

·1 cup grated white radish

·2 green onions, into thin strips

·4 garlic cloves minced

·2 slices fresh ginger

·1 tsp white sugar

·1 tsp salt

·1 tsp white vinegar

·3 pinches of red pepper threads dried,
Korean

DIRECTIONS

1. Bring the apples and vinegar to a boil in a stockpot. Reduce heat to low and cook, uncovered, for 30 to 40 minutes or until vegetables are soft. Remove from the heat and let it cool slightly. In a food processor, mix in batches until smooth. Return everything to the pan.

2. Sugar, brown sugar, salt, cinnamon, extract, cloves, & allspice are combined in a bowl. Red hots should be dissolved in boiling water and then added to the apple mixture.

3. Bring the water to a boil. Reduce heat to low and cook, uncovered, for 2 hours or until the mixture has thickened to a spreadable consistency.

4. Remove the pan from the heat. Carefully spoon the heated mixture into 8 1-pint sterilized jars, allowing ¼-inch headspace. Remove air bubbles and, if required, correct the headspace by adding a heated mixture. Clean the rims. Screw on bands till the fingertip is tight; center lids on jars.

5. Place the jars in a canner filled with simmering water, ensuring they are fully covered. Bring to a boil, then reduce to a simmer for 5 minutes. Remove the jars and set them aside to cool.

NUTRITION

Calories: 27 Kcal	Protein: 1.7 g
Carbohydrates: 5.6 g	Fat: 0.3 g

98.

SPICY PICKLED CAULIFLOWER

🥣 3 Pints   🍴 Prep Time : 10 Mins   🕐 Cook Time : 5 Mins

INGREDIENTS

BRINE

- 2 cups water
- 1 cup seasoned rice vinegar
- ¼ cup white sugar
- 2 tbsp kosher salt
- 1 tsp ground turmeric

CAULIFLOWER PICKLE

- 1 (2 lb)cauliflower, cut into florets
- 1½ tsp kosher salt
- 9 small Thai chili peppers
- 6 garlic cloves, peeled
- 2 tsp whole black peppercorns

DIRECTIONS

1.   In a saucepan, combine the water, sugar, rice vinegar, salt, and turmeric. Cook, occasionally stirring, until the sugar & salt have dissolved, approximately 5 minutes. Remove the pan from the heat and put it aside.

2.   In a bowl, sprinkle cauliflower florets with kosher salt and set them aside for 30 minutes.

3.   Rinse the cauliflower and equally divide the florets, garlic cloves, chili peppers, and black peppercorns among 3 pint-sized jars, pushing down to make sure everything is packed snugly. Fill the jars halfway with brine and cover the cauliflower with it.

4.   Before serving, put the lids on the jars and place them in the refrigerator to marinate for 2 to 3 days. In approximately a week, the flavor will be at its finest.

NUTRITION

Calories: 47 Kcal	Protein: 2.1 g
Carbohydrates: 11 g	Fat: 0.2 g

DILL PICKLE SANDWICH SLICES

 3 Pints   Prep Time : 10 Mins   Cook Time : 20 Mins

INGREDIENTS

- ·2 tbsp mixed pickling spice
- ·2½ cups cider vinegar
- ·2½ cups water
- ·½ cup granulated sugar
- ·⅓ cup preserving & pickling salt
- ·3 bay leaves
- ·3 garlic cloves
- ·1½ tsp mustard seeds
- ·3 heads fresh dill
- ·8 cups (¼-inch slices)sliced, pickling cucumbers

DIRECTIONS

1. As specified in the step-by-step instructions, prepare the stockpot/canner and jars.

2. Make a spice bag by tying pickling spices in a square of cheesecloth.

3. In a medium stainless steel saucepan, combine the water, vinegar, sugar, pickling salt, & spice bag. Over medium-high heat, bring to a boil, constantly stirring to dissolve the sugar and salt. Reduce heat to low and continue to cook for 15 minutes, or until the spices have fully permeated the liquid.

4. Fill each jar with 1 bay leaf, ½ tsp mustard seeds, 1 garlic clove, and 1 dill head. Fill heated jars halfway with cucumber slices, allowing ½ inch headspace. tsp pickle crisp granulates, rounded. Fill jars halfway with hot pickling liquid, allowing ½ inch headspace. Re-measure headspace after removing air bubbles. Add additional cucumbers if necessary to get the desired headspace. Wipe the rim and place the lid in the middle of the jar. Screw the band on until it is fingertip tight.

5. Fill jars halfway with water and boil for 15 minutes.

6. Remove the lid from the stockpot. Wait 5 minutes before removing the jars, cooling them, and storing them.

NUTRITION

Calories: 29 Kcal	Protein: 0.3 g
Carbohydrates: 5.2 g	Fat: 0.1 g

100.

BAKED MUSHROOM & ONION OMELET

 8 Pints | Prep Time : 5 Mins | Cook Time : 10 Mins

INGREDIENTS

- 1 red bell pepper
- 1 onion
- 1 tsp olive oil
- 1 portabella mushroom
- 8 egg whites
- 1-cup baby spinach
- cup mozzarella cheese
- 5 eggs
- Salt & pepper for taste

DIRECTIONS

1. Preheat the oven to 350 °F. Using olive oil, grease all insides of 6 12-pint canning jars. In a medium-sized pan, heat the olive oil over medium-low heat.

2. Cook for approximately 15 to 30 minutes, or until the onions are light golden brown.

3. Cook until the veggies are tender, then add the portabella mushroom and pepper. Remove from the heat and set aside to cool.

4. Toss the eggs with a sprinkle of salt to taste.

5. In the canning jars, evenly distribute the eggs, cooked veggies, and baby spinach. Finish with a sprinkling of cheese.

6. Bake for 30 minutes or until the eggs are fully done. It's best served hot.

NUTRITION

Calories: 130 Kcal | Protein: 15 g

Carbohydrates: 6 g | Fat: 5 g

CANNED TOMATOES

🥣 6   🍴 **Prep Time : 20 Mins**   🕐 **Cook Time : 90 Mins**

INGREDIENTS

- 9 lbs ripe peeled and halved tomatoes
- ½ tbsp lemon juice
- ½ tbsp salt in each jar

DIRECTIONS

1. Pack the tomatoes in the sterilized jars while pressing them down so that the space between the tomato pieces is filled with their juices.
2. Leave a ½-inch headspace.
3. Add a tbsp lemon juice and ½ tbsp salt to each jar.
4. Rinse the rims and place the lids and the rings on the jars.
5. Can them in the pressure canner for 90 minutes at 10 lb pressure.
6. Wait for the pressure canner to depressurize to remove the jars. Place the jars on a cooling rack, then store them in a cool, dry place.

NUTRITION

Calories: 13 Kcal	Fat: 0 g	Protein: 1 g
Cholesterol: 0 mg	Carbohydrates: 3 g	Sugar:17.93 g

102.

PICCALILLI

🥣 4   ✂️ **Prep Time : 20 Mins**   🕐 **Cook Time : 40 Mins**

INGREDIENTS

- 2 quarts green tomatoes
- ½ cup pickling salt
- Pint white vinegar
- ¼ cup mustard seed
- 1 tsp cinnamon
- 1 tsp dry mustard
- 1 tsp allspice
- 1 tsp ground cloves
- 1 tsp celery seed
- ½ tsp pepper
- 2 green peppers
- 2 chopped onions
- 3 cups sugar

DIRECTIONS

1. Chop tomatoes in a meat grinder, using a coarse blade. Sprinkle with salt, press down, and let stand. Cover and keep overnight in a cool place. Drain well.

2. Combine vinegar and spices in a large pot and bring to a boil. Seed and chop the peppers and onion.

3. Add vegetables and sugar to a kettle, and bring to a boil. Simmer for 30 minutes, stirring as needed. Package the hot relish into sterilized, hot jars, allowing ¼ inch of headspace. Wipe the jar's rim; set a warm lid in place and tighten.

4. Place in a bath canner with boiling water and process for 15 minutes.

NUTRITION

Calories: 16 Kcal	Fat: 0 g	Protein: 0.1 g
Cholesterol: 0 mg	Carbohydrates: 1.9 g	Sugar: 83.75 g

SPLIT PEA SOUP

🍜 2   ✕ **Prep Time : 20 Mins**   🕐 **Cook Time : 90 Mins**

INGREDIENTS

- 1 lb yellow, dry split peas
- 2 quarts water
- 4 tsp lime juice
- ¾ cup sliced carrots
- 1 cup chopped onions
- 2 minced garlic cloves
- ½ tsp cayenne pepper
- 1 tsp cumin seed and coriander
- 1 tsp salt

DIRECTIONS

1. Allow the water with split peas in it to come to a boil in a large stockpot. Let it gently simmer without covering until the peas become soft; this will take about an hour.

2. Add the other ingredients and allow it to continue simmering for 30 minutes more. Check the consistency and thin out the water if necessary.

3. Ladle it into jars and leave a headspace of 1 inch. Put a cap on and seal. Put it in a canner with hot water of 2 to 3 inches and allow a processing time of 90 minutes at high pressure.

NUTRITION

Calories: 158 Kcal	Fat: 2.8 g	Protein: 8.3 g
Cholesterol: 0 mg	Carbohydrates: 26 g	Sugar: 8.05 g

104.

APPLE RELISH

 4 · Prep Time : 20 Mins · Cook Time : 20 Mins

INGREDIENTS

- ·4 lb apples
- ·3 quarts water
- ·1 ¼ cup white vinegar, divided
- ·1 cup sugar
- ·½ cup light corn syrup
- · cup water
- ·2 tsp whole cloves
- ·1 ½ stick cinnamon

DIRECTIONS

1. Wash, pare, and core, and then cut the apples into eighths. Place them in a bowl containing 3 quarts of water and 4 tbsp vinegar to prevent darkening.

2. Combine sugar, corn syrup, the rest of the vinegar, cup water, cloves, and cinnamon (broken into pieces) in a pot. Heat to boiling. Drain apples and add to the pot. Cover and boil for 3 minutes, stirring occasionally.

3. Ladle into hot, sterilized jars, leaving ¼ inch of headspace. Fill with syrup, still being sure to leave ¼ inch of headspace. Wipe the jar's rim; set a warm lid in place and tighten. Place in a bath canner with boiling water and process for 10 minutes.

NUTRITION

Calories: 53.1 Kcal	Fat: 0.2 g	Protein: 0.3 g
Cholesterol: 0 mg	Carbohydrates: 15.8 g	Sugar: 1 04.6 g

CANNED MANGOS

🥣 6   ✂️ **Prep Time : 10 Mins**   🕐 **Cook Time : 30 Mins**

INGREDIENTS

·8 mangoes, peeled, seeded & cut into chunks

·4 tbsp sugar

·3 tbsp fresh lemon juice

2 cups water

DIRECTIONS

1. Pack mangoes into the jars. Leave ½-inch headspace.
2. Add 1 tbsp lemon juice to each jar.
3. Add 2 cups water and sugar in a pot and bring to a boil. Stir until sugar is dissolved.
4. Pour hot sugar syrup over the mangoes.
5. Seal jar with lids. Process in a water bath canner for 15 minutes.
6. Remove jars from the water bath and let them cool completely.
7. Check the seals of jars. Label and store.

NUTRITION

Calories: 300 Kcal	Fat: 2 g	Sugar: 70 g
Cholesterol: 0 mg	Carbohydrates: 75 g	Protein: 3 g

106.

TOMATO JUICE

 4 Quarts   Prep Time : 15 Mins   Cook Time : 55 Mins

INGREDIENTS

- 14 lb tomatoes, cored and quartered
- 1 tbsp salt
- ½ cup / 120ml lemon Juice, bottled

DIRECTIONS

1. Take 6 quarts or 6l stainless steel stockpot or Dutch oven. Add tomatoes cored and diced into small pieces and allow them to boil. Stir occasionally.
2. Reduce the flame and let it simmer uncovered for about 15 minutes or more until it becomes soft.
3. Take a food mill and press the tomato mixture in different batches and transfer it into a large bowl. Discard tomato skin and seeds.
4. Transfer the tomato puree to the Dutch oven again and bring it to a boil at a medium flame with frequent stirring until the temperature reaches 88°C. Remove from the flame. Add lemon juice and stir well.
5. Transfer the hot tomato juice into a hot jar with a ladle. Leave a 1-inch space on the top. Remove air bubbles. Clean the rim of the glass jar.
6. Place the lid and apply a band around it. Adjust to ensure that the lid is tight. Place the jar in the boiling water bath canner. Leave the water bath canner for about 40 minutes.
7. Turn off the canner and remove the lid. Keep the jars in the canner for 5 minutes more. Remove the jars, then allow them to cool. Store in the refrigerator.

NUTRITION

Calories: 50 Kcal	Fat: 0 g
Carbohydrates: 10 g	Protein: 2 g

TOMATO PASTE

🥣 **16 Pints**   **Prep Time : 15 Mins**   **Cook Time : 3H 35 Mins**

INGREDIENTS

- 16 lb plum/paste tomatoes, cubed
- 3 cups sweet pepper, chopped
- 2 bay leaves
- 2 tbsp salt
- 3 garlic cloves
- 6 tbsp lemon juice, bottled

DIRECTIONS

1. In a 6L pot, mix all ingredients and cook on a medium flame for an hour with continuous stirring.

2. Remove bay leaves. Strain the mixture using a sieve. Return the mixture to your pot and cook for 3 hours over a medium-low flame with frequent stirring.

3. Transfer the hot jam into a hot jar with a ladle. Leave ½ inch of space on the top. Remove air bubbles. Clean the rim of the glass jar.

4. Place the lid and apply a band around it. Adjust to ensure that the lid is tight. Place the jar in the water bath canner that has boiling water.

Leave the water bath canner for about 30 minutes. Turn off the canner and remove the lid. Keep the jars in the canner for 5 minutes more. Remove the jars then allow them to cool. Store in the refrigerator.

NUTRITION

Calories: 30 Kcal   Fat: 0 g

Carbohydrates: 6 g   Protein: 1 g

108.

CANNED HONEY AND CINNAMON PEACHES

 7 Pints   Prep Time : 15 Mins   Cook Time : 30 Mins

INGREDIENTS

- 3 lb ripe peaches
- 1 cup honey
- 7 cinnamon sticks

DIRECTIONS

1. Peel the peaches and dunk them in boiling water for 2 minutes. The skin will then come off. Meanwhile, mix 9 cups of water and honey, and bring the mixture to a boil over medium heat.

2. Place a cinnamon stick in each sterilized pint jar. Pack the peaches in the jars and add the honey mixture, leaving some space. Clean the jar rims and adjust the lids.

3. Transfer the jars to the pressure canner with water so that the jars are covered by water at least 2 inches.

4. Cover the pressure canner with an ordinary lid that fits well and process the pint jars for 30 minutes in the boiling water.

NUTRITION

Calories: 70 Kcal   Fat: 0 g

Carbohydrates: 17 g   Protein: 0 g

HONEY-LAVENDER PEACHES

🥣 12 Pints	✕ Prep Time : 15 Mins	🕐 Cook Time : 70 Mins

INGREDIENTS

- ·15 lb ripe peaches
- ·4 cups water
- ·1 ¾ cup honey
- · cup Riesling
- ·1 tbsp lavender buds, dried
- ·½ tbsp salt
- ·1 lemon

DIRECTIONS

1. Boil a large pot of water. Cook the peaches, in batches, in the boiling water for 60 seconds or until the skin starts to peel.

2. Use a slotted spoon for removing the peaches from the hot water and into a large bowl of ice-cold water. Peel the peaches after removing them from the cold water.

3. Remove the pits then slice them in half lengthwise. Make the syrup by combining 4 cups of water, honey, Riesling, lavender buds, and salt in a large saucepan.

4. Cook over medium-high heat as you stir until the honey has all dissolved. Cut 3 inches strips of lemon peel using a vegetable peeler. Reserve the lemon for other use.

5. Pack the peaches in the jars with the cut side facing down. Add the lemon peel, then spoon the syrup evenly among the jars leaving a ½-inch headspace.

6. Rinse the jar rims and place the lids and rings on the jars. Transfer the jars to the pressure canner and process at 10 lb pressure for 70 minutes.

7. Let the canner rest to cool before removing the jars and placing them on a rack to cool.

NUTRITION

Calories: 60 Kcal Fat: 0 g

Carbohydrates: 17 g Protein: 1 g

110.

SPICED APPLE RINGS

 8 Pints   **Prep Time : 15 Mins**   **Cook Time : 50 Mins**

INGREDIENTS

- 12 lb green apples
- 8 cups white sugar
- 6 cups water
- 1¼ cup white vinegar
- 3 tbsp whole cloves
- 8 cinnamon sticks

DIRECTIONS

1. Wash, core, peel, and slice the apples. The thickness needs to be small-medium to fit into the jar. In a large saucepan, combine sugar, water, vinegar, cloves, and cinnamon sticks.

2. Boil as you stir until the sugar is dissolved. Then lower the heat and let simmer for 3 minutes. Add the apples to the saucepan and cook for about 5 minutes.

3. Place the apples and syrup into the jars equally.

4. Process pint or quart jars at 10 lb for 45 minutes for the weighted gauge of the pressure canner or 11 lb if the pressure canner has a dial gauge.

5. Remove jars and let cool until at room temperature before storing. This may take about a day.

NUTRITION

Calories: 35 Kcal	Fat: 0 g
Carbohydrates: 9 g	Protein: 0 g

148

PICKLED PLUMS

🥣 **5 Pints**   ✂ **Prep Time : 35 Mins**   🕐 **Cook Time : 60 Mins**

INGREDIENTS

· 3-½ lb red/ green or purple plums

· 2 onions

· 2 cups water

· 2 cups red wine vinegar

· 2-½ cups sugar

· 3 inches cinnamon sticks

· 8 whole allspices

· 4 garlic cloves

· ½ tbsp salt

· 2 star anise

DIRECTIONS

1. Wash the plums thoroughly with water and rinse them. Trim off its roots and stems from the onions, then cut them into ½-inch pieces. Pack the plums and onions in sterilized jars.

2. Combine water and wine vinegar in a saucepan and bring the mixture to a boil. In a saucepan, stir in sugar, cinnamon sticks, allspice, garlic cloves, salt, and star anise.

3. Let the mixture boil until the sugar has dissolved. Remove the mixture from the heat. Pour the hot mixture on the jars with plums, leaving a ¼-inch headspace.

4. Wipe the jar rims and place the lids and rings on the jar. Process the jars in the pressure canner for 40 minutes at 10 lb pressure.

5. Wait for the pressure canner to depressurize to zero before removing the jars and cooling them on a wire rack for 12 to 24 hours.

NUTRITION

Calories: 239 Kcal	Carbohydrates: 59 g
Fat: 0 g	Protein: 1 g

112.

CANNED PORT AND CINNAMON PLUMS

 7 Pints | Prep Time : 25 Mins | Cook Time : 80 Mins

INGREDIENTS

- ·4–½ lb plums
- ·1 orange
- ·4 cups water
- ·2–½ cups sugar
- ·¾ cup ruby port
- ·¼ tbsp salt
- ·7 3-inch cinnamon sticks

DIRECTIONS

1. Quarter the plums and pit them. Cut 3 inches of strips from the orange peel. Squeeze cup juice from your orange

2. Make the syrup by adding the orange juice in a saucepan, then add all other ingredients except the cinnamon sticks. Bring the mixture to a boil and stir to dissolve all sugar.

3. Pack the plums, orange strips, and cinnamon sticks in the sterilized jars. Ladle the syrup leaving a ½-inch headspace. Wipe the rims; place the lids and the rings on the jars.

4. Process the jars in the pressure canner for 70 minutes at 10 lb pressure.

5. Let the pressure canner depressurize to zero to remove the jars. Transfer the jar to a wire rack and let it cool for 24 hours before storing them.

NUTRITION

Calories: 125 Kcal

Fat: 0 g

Carbohydrates: 30 g

Protein: 1 g

SWEET GREEN TOMATO KETCHUP

🍚 16   ✗ Prep Time : 25 Mins   🕐 Cook Time : 35 Mins

INGREDIENTS

- ·5 green tomatoes, chopped
- ·1 red bell pepper, seeded and chopped
- ·1 white onion, chopped
- ·½ cup pickling salt
- ·1 cup white vinegar
- · cup packed brown sugar
- ·1 tsp ground cinnamon
- ·1 tsp pumpkin pie spice
- ·10 tbsp white sugar
- ·8 whole cloves
- ·1 tbsp dark corn syrup

DIRECTIONS

1. In a large bowl, layer the tomatoes, bell peppers, and onion, seasoning each layer with salt as you go. Keep making layers until you run out of vegetables. Cover the bowl and refrigerate for 4 to 5 hours.

2. Pour the vegetables into a colander and rinse off the salt under running water.

3. Put them into a pot with a lid and stir the vinegar, brown sugar, cinnamon, pumpkin pie spice, white sugar, whole cloves, and corn syrup. Bring to a boil, and then simmer over medium heat, uncovered, for about 30 minutes. The tomatoes will start to turn pale.

4. When the vegetables are very soft, press them through a sieve, being sure to find all of the cloves and remove them. Cool the sauce and store it in the refrigerator.

NUTRITION

Calories: 85 Kcal	Carbohydrates: 21.3 g	Sodium: 3470.6 mg
Protein: 0.7 g	Fat: 0.1 g	

114.

TOMATO SOUP

 5 Quarts   Prep Time : 15 Mins   Cook Time : 85 Mins

INGREDIENTS

- ·12 lb tomatoes, quartered cut
- ·1 tbsp sugar
- ·2 tbsp pickling spices
- ·2 tbsp salt
- ·1 tsp peppercorns
- ·4 onions, medium-sized, chopped
- ·2 carrots, sliced

DIRECTIONS

1. Take a 6L pot and add tomatoes, sugar, onions, and carrots. Tie pickling spices, salt, and peppercorns in a cheesecloth bag. Place it in the pot.

2. Bring the mixture to a boil on a medium-high flame. Reduce the flame and let it simmer for 45 minutes or more until it becomes thick. Remove the spice bag. Strain the soup and boil it again.

3. Transfer the hot soup into a hot jar with a ladle. Leave½ inch of space on the top. Remove air bubbles. Clean the rim of the glass jar.

4. Place the lid and apply a band around it. Adjust to ensure that the lid is tight. Place the jar in the water bath canner that has boiling water. Leave the water bath canner for about 40 minutes.

5. Turn off the canner and remove the lid. Keep the jars in the canner for 5 minutes more. Remove the jars and allow them to cool. Store in the refrigerator.

NUTRITION

Calories: 90 Kcal   Fat: 0 g

Carbohydrates: 20 g   Protein: 2 g

PERSIMMON BUTTER

 5 Pints | Prep Time : 15 Mins | Cook Time : 15 Mins

INGREDIENTS

·8 cups persimmon purée
·1 cup orange juice
·1 ½ cup honey
·1 orange grated zest

DIRECTIONS

1.Combine all the ingredients in a large stockpot; cook over medium-high heat until thick, about 10 to 15 minutes.

Ladle into sterilized jars, leaving ¼" headspace. Wipe rims, cap, and seal. Process in a water-bath canner for 10 minutes

NUTRITION

Calories: 14 Kcal   Fat: 0 g
Carbohydrates: 4 g   Protein: 0 g

116.

BERRY BLISS

🥣 **4 Pints**   **Prep Time : 15 Mins**   **Cook Time : 15 Mins**

INGREDIENTS

· 4 cups Monin sugar syrup
· 8 cups mixed fresh berries

DIRECTIONS

1. Wash berries in cold water; remove any bruised spots. Heat sugar syrup to boiling; fill each jar with ½ cup liquid. Add berries, leaving ½" headspace and making sure berries are covered in liquid.

2. Remove any air bubbles. Put on lids; process for 15 minutes in a hot-water bath.

NUTRITION

Calories: 61 Kcal	Fat: 0 g
Carbohydrates: 10 g	Protein: 1 g

LEMON ZESTY PEARS

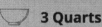 **3 Quarts**   **Prep Time : 15 Mins**   **Cook Time : 15 Mins**

INGREDIENTS

· 8 lb pears

· ¼ tsp Fruit Fresh

· 2 cups sugar

· tsp grated lemon zest for every 3 lb pears

· 4 cups water

DIRECTIONS

1.   Wash pears and drain. Peel, core, and halve or quarter. Treat with Fruit Fresh mixed in water to prevent darkening.

2.   To make syrup, in a large stockpot, combine sugar, lemon zest, and water; stir well. Heat until boiling; reduce heat to medium. Cook pears until they are tender, 5 to 6 minutes. Ladle hot pears into sterilized jars, leaving ½" headspace.

3.   Ladle hot syrup over pears, leaving ½" headspace. Wipe rims; cap and seal. Process in a water-bath canner for 20 minutes for pints or 25 minutes for quarts.

NUTRITION

Calories: 120 Kcal	Fat: 4 g
Carbohydrates: 16 g	Protein: 0 g

CHAPTER 7: JELLY AND SYRUP

118.

LEMON & WINE JELLY

🥣 40   ✕ **Prep Time : 10 Mins**   🕐 **Cook Time : 30 Mins**

INGREDIENTS

- ½ cup fresh lemon juice
- 3 ½ cups wine
- 4 ½ cups white sugar
- 2 oz dry pectin

DIRECTIONS

1. In a pot, combine lemon juice, wine, and pectin and bring to a gentle boil.
2. Stir in sugar and cook for about 2 minutes.
3. Skim off the foam and ladle it into sterile jars.

Seal and process in a hot water bath for about 5 minutes

NUTRITION

Calories: 106 Kcal	Total Fat: 0 g	Dietary Fiber: 0 g	Protein: 0 g
Cholesterol: 0 mg	Carbohydrates: 23.4 g	Sugar: 22.7 g	Sodium: 1 mg

PLUM JELLY

🥣 16   ✂ **Prep Time : 10 Mins**   🕐 **Cook Time : 50 Mins**

INGREDIENTS

·6 large pineapples, peeled, cored & cut into chunks

·5 cups water

·1 cup sugar

DIRECTIONS

1. Add plums and water to a large saucepan and bring to a boil. Cover and simmer over medium heat for 10 minutes.

2. Strain the plum juice by straining it through a mesh strainer. Let drain for 30 minutes. Discard plums.

3. You will get 5 ½ cups of plum juice.

4. Pour the juice into the pot. Add pectin and stir well and bring to a boil.

5. Add sugar and boil jelly for 1 minute.

6. Remove pot from heat.

7. Ladle jelly into the clean jars. Leave ½-inch headspace. Remove air bubbles.

8. Seal jars with lids and process in a boiling water bath for 10 minutes.

9. Remove jars from the water bath and let them cool completely.

10. Check the seals of jars. Label and store.

NUTRITION

Calories: 320 Kcal	Carbohydrates: 83.8 g	Protein: 0.2 g
Fat: 0.8 g	Sugar: 83.4 g	Cholesterol: 2 mg

120.

STRAWBERRY PRESERVES

 10   Prep Time : 10 Mins   Cook Time : 20 Mins

INGREDIENTS

- ·2 lb strawberries
- ·2 tbsp vinegar
- ·5 cups sugar
- ·Pinch of salt

DIRECTIONS

1.   Add all ingredients into the stockpot and bring to a boil.
2.   Stir frequently and cook for 15 to 20 minutes.
3.   Remove pot from heat.
4.   Ladle strawberry preserves into the clean jars, leaving ½–inch headspace.
5.   Remove air bubbles.
6.   Seal jars with lids and process in a boiling water bath for 10 minutes.
7.   Remove jars from the water bath and let them cool completely.
8.   Check the seals of jars. Label and store.

NUTRITION

Calories: 405 Kcal	Fat: 0.3 g	Sugar: 1045 g
Cholesterol: 0 mg	Carbohydrates: 107 g	Protein: 0.6 g

PRESERVED FIGS

🥣 14   ✂️ **Prep Time : 10 Mins**   🕐 **Cook Time : 45 Mins**

INGREDIENTS

- ·6 cups figs, trimmed & roughly cut
- ·1 packet liquid pectin
- ·1 tsp butter
- ·1 tsp lime zest
- ·¼ cup lime juice
- ·½ cup water
- ·7 cups sugar

DIRECTIONS

1. Add all ingredients except liquid pectin into the large pot and let sit for 30 minutes.
2. After 30 minutes, place a pot on heat and bring to a boil. Boil for 10 minutes.
3. Stir in liquid pectin. Stir constantly for 1 minute.
4. Remove the pot from the heat and let it cool slightly.
5. Ladle figs into the clean jars, leaving ½-inch headspace. Remove air bubbles.
6. Seal jars with lids and process in a boiling water bath for 20 minutes.
7. Remove jars from the water bath and let them cool completely.
8. Check the seals of jars. Label and store.

NUTRITION

Calories: 591 Kcal	Fat: 1.1 g	Sugar: 140.9 g
Cholesterol: 0 mg	Carbohydrates: 154.6 g	Protein: 2.8 g

122.

GRAPE JELLY

 32   ✂ **Prep Time : 30 Mins**   🕐 **Cook Time : 30 Mins**

INGREDIENTS

- 3½ lb grapes
- ½ (6 fluid oz) container of liquid pectin
- 7 cups white sugar
- ½ cup water

DIRECTIONS

1. Wash the grapes and crush them in a large bowl; transfer to a pan and add in water.
2. Bring to a boil and then simmer for about 10 minutes; remove from heat and then extract the juice.
3. Let the juice cool overnight.
4. Strain the juice into a pot and stir in sugar.
5. Bring to a boil and then remove from heat.
6. Divide among the sterile jars and process for about 5 minutes in a hot water bath.
7. Refrigerate.

NUTRITION

Calories: 101 Kcal   Carbohydrates: 26.2 g   Sugar: 25.9 g   Sodium: 0.7 mg

Total Fat: 0.1 g   Dietary Fiber: 0.3 g   Protein: 0.2 g

LEMON & POMEGRANATE JELLY

🥣 96　　✕ Prep Time : 30 Mins　　🕐 Cook Time : 30 Mins

INGREDIENTS

- 4 cups pomegranate juice
- 2 lemons, juiced
- 6 fluid oz liquid pectin
- 7½ cups white sugar

DIRECTIONS

1. In a large pan, combine lemon juice, pomegranate, and sugar, and bring to a rolling boil; stir in pectin and simmer for about 1 minute. Ladle the jelly into sterile jars and seal. Process in a hot water bath and then refrigerate.

NUTRITION

Calories: 43 Kcal	Total Fat: 0 g	Dietary Fiber: 0.1 g	Protein: 0 g
Cholesterol: 0 mg	Carbohydrates: 11.6 g	Sugars: 11.1 g	Sodium: 0.1 mg

124.

ELDERBERRY JELLY

🥣 5   ✂ Prep Time : 10 Mins   🕐 Cook Time : 35 Mins

INGREDIENTS

- 4 lb crushed elderberries
- 1 packet of pectin
- ¼ cup lemon juice
- ¼ tsp butter
- 4 ½ cups sugar

DIRECTIONS

1. Add the crushed elderberries to a pot.
2. Place the pot on the stove over medium heat. Bring the elderberries to a boil while continuing to crush them.
3. Simmer for 10 minutes before removing the pot from the stove.
4. Strain the mixture through a sieve held over a clean pot. You want the juice of the berries to go into the pot.
5. Add the pectin following the instructions on the packet. Stir in the lemon juice.
6. Boil and stir in the butter and sugar. Continue constantly stirring until the jelly reaches a rolling boil. Continue to boil for 2 minutes.
7. Pour the jelly into the jars, leaving about ¼ an inch of space in each jar. Attach the lids.
8. Process the jars using the water bath canning method for 5 to 10 minutes.

NUTRITION

Calories: 50 Kcal   TotalCarbohydrates: 13 g

Total Fat: 0 g   Proteins: 0 g

PEACH JELLY

 3   Prep Time : 10 Mins   Cook Time : 35 Mins

INGREDIENTS

- ·4 sliced peaches
- ·2 cups white sugar
- ·2 tbsp pectin
- ·5 green tea bags
- ·2 cups water

DIRECTIONS

1. Mix the white sugar with the water in a pot. Place the pot on the stove and bring the mixture to a simmer. While stirring, let the mixture simmer until the sugar has dissolved completely.

2. Place 4 green tea bags into the mixture and let simmer for about 5 minutes.

3. Carefully remove the 4 tea bags from the pot. Stir in the peaches and continue to simmer for 10 more minutes. Taste the mixture every so often until it reaches the desired flavor intensity.

4. Strain the mixture through a sieve. Place the liquid syrup back into the pot. Stir in the pectin and bring the syrup to a rolling boil.

5. Keep boiling until the syrup reaches 220°F.

6. Pour the peach jelly into the jars.

7. Attach the lids and process using the water bath canning method for 10 minutes.

NUTRITION

Calories: 10 Kcal   Total Carbohydrates: 5 g

Total Fat: 0 g   Proteins: 0 g

126.

SAVORY RUBY PORT VINEGAR JELLY

🥣 4   ✂ Prep Time : 10 Mins   🕐 Cook Time : 30 Mins

INGREDIENTS

- ·¼ cup orange peel, shredded
- · cup balsamic vinegar
- ·3 cups sugar
- ·1 pack of liquid fruit pectin
- ·2 cups ruby port

DIRECTIONS

1. To make the jelly, take a heavy saucepan; mix in the orange peel and vinegar.
2. Keep the heat on a medium setting; let the mixture heat for about 4 to 5 minutes.
3. Remove the peel from the hot mixture.
4. Place the vinegar mixture back in the saucepan and add the port and sugar.
5. Keep the heat on a high setting; then add the pectin and continue boiling for about 1-2 more minutes.
6. Then remove it from the heat; remove the foam using a spoon.
7. After that, take the pre-sterilized jars; place the jelly mixture into the jars.
8. Keep ½" margin from the top.
9. Use a damp cloth to clean jar rims; then close them with the lid and band.
10. Afterward, place the jars in the canning pot filled with water.
11. Set the canning timer at 10 minutes; adjust the canning time based on your altitude level.
12. After the canning time is over, take out the hot jars, wipe them and take off the bands.
13. Store in a dry, cool area and enjoy the delicious jelly.

NUTRITION

Calories: 65.1 Kcal   Total Carbohydrates: 93 g

Total Fat: 2.6 g   Protein: 1.7 g

CHERRIES IN SYRUP

 9 Pint Jars   Prep Time : 30 Mins   Cook Time : 60 Mins

INGREDIENTS

·11 lb cherries

COLOR PRESERVATIVE SOLUTION:

·½ cup lemon juice mixed with ½ gallon water or ascorbic acid per label

·5 ½ cups water and 2 ½ cups sugar (for sweet cherries) or 5 cups water and 3 ¼ cups sugar (for sour cherries)

DIRECTIONS

1. Before pitting the cherries, wash them and remove the stems. Place the cherries in the color preservative solution while the water is heating up. Bring the sugar and water to a boil, then add the drained cherries and reheat to a boil. Fill jars to within ½ inch of the rim with cherries and syrup. Remove the bubbles, wash the rim, and process the lids on top.

2. Pitting cherries is a messy task, no matter how you do it. Because cherry juice stains, use an apron or old clothing. If you don't have a cherry pitter, there are instructions on making one on the sidebar. The stem tips of pitted cherries will discolor if not dipped into the color preservative solution as they are pitted.

3. Half-frozen cherries are simpler to pit and less messy. Place little portions of fruit in the freezer for 30 minutes before pitting. If you cook cherries for too long, they will lose their color and shape; bring the syrup and cherries to a boil. Before filling the jars, a few drops of red food coloring may be added to the cherries if desired.

4. Try to acquire an equal number of cherries and syrup in each jar. The cherries will settle to the bottom if there is too much syrup; if required, add one smaller jar to make the jars seem full.

NUTRITION

Calories: 32 Kcal	Fat: 0 g
Carbohydrates: 21 g	Protein: 0 g

128.

RASPBERRY SYRUP

 5 Jars　　 Prep Time : 15 Mins　　🕐 Cook Time : 5 Mins

INGREDIENTS

- ·3 lb raspberries
- ·2 cups water
- ·2 layers of cheesecloth
- ·2¾ cups (675 mL) sugar
- ·½ cup light corn syrup
- ·2 tbsp lemon juice

DIRECTIONS

1.　In a 6-qt. (6-L) stainless steel or enameled Dutch oven, combine raspberries and water. Over medium-low heat, bring to a simmer. Cook for 20 minutes, uncovered, stirring periodically. (Do not bring to a boil.) Remove the pan from the heat. 2 layers of moistened cheesecloth or a jelly bag should be used to line a wire-mesh strainer. Place a bowl on top of it. Pour the berry mixture into a strainer and drain for 2 hours or as required to get 412 cups (1.13 L) of juice. (Do not squeeze or force the mixture.) Solids should be discarded. Clean the Dutch oven.

2.　In a Dutch oven, combine the raspberry juice, sugar, and the next 2 ingredients, stirring until the sugar dissolves. Over medium-high heat, bring the mixture to a full rolling boil; cook for 1 minute. Fill a heated jar halfway with hot syrup, allowing a 12-inch (1-cm) headspace. Air bubbles should be removed. Wipe the jar's rim. On the jar, place the lid in the middle. Apply the band and tighten it until it is fingertip-tight. In a boiling-water canner, place the jar. Repeat until all of the jars are full.

3.　Adjust for altitude and process jars for 10 minutes. Remove jars from heat, remove lids, and set aside for 5 minutes. Remove the jars and set them aside to cool.

NUTRITION

Calories: 30 Kcal	Fat: 3 g
Carbohydrates: 11 g	Protein: 0 g

TART CHERRIES IN GINGER SYRUP

🍵 **5 Jars** ✂️ **Prep Time : 15 Mins** **Cook Time : 5 Mins**

INGREDIENTS

- ·6 cups water
- ·2 cups sugar
- ·1 cup ginger slices
- ·2½ lb tart cherries

DIRECTIONS

1. In a 6-qt. (6-L) stainless steel or enameled Dutch oven, bring the first 3 ingredients to a boil; decrease heat and simmer, uncovered, for 1 hour or until syrupy. Using a slotted spoon, transfer ginger slices to a bowl. 3 cups of syrup should be leftover (750 mL). Toss cherries into the syrup. Bring to a boil, then reduce to low heat and cook for 5 minutes, or until well heated.

2. Fill a heated jar halfway with hot cherries and syrup, then top with several slices of shaved ginger and a 12-inch (1 cm) headspace. Air bubbles should be removed. Wipe the jar's rim. On the jar, place the lid in the middle. Apply the band and tighten it until it is fingertip-tight. In a boiling-water canner, place the jar. Rep until all of the jars are full. Adjust for altitude and process jars for 10 minutes. Remove jars from heat, remove lids, and set aside for 5 minutes. Remove the jars and set them aside to cool.

NUTRITION

Calories: 24 Kcal   Fat: 1 g

Carbohydrates: 21 g   Protein: 3 g

130.

STRAWBERRY SYRUP

 5 Jars   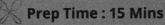 Prep Time : 15 Mins   Cook Time : 5 Mins

INGREDIENTS

- 3 ½ lb strawberries
- 3 cups water
- 1 cinnamon stick
- 2 layers of cheesecloth
- 6 cups sugar
- ¾ cup light corn syrup
- cup bottled lemon juice

DIRECTIONS

1. In a 6-qt. (6-L) stainless steel or enameled Dutch oven, combine the first 3 ingredients. Over medium-low heat, bring to a simmer. Cook for 20 minutes, uncovered, stirring periodically. (Do not bring to a boil.) Remove the pan from the heat. To line a wire mesh strainer, use 2 layers of moistened cheesecloth or a jelly bag. Place a bowl on top of it. Pour the berry combination into the sieve and drain for 2 hours or as required to get 6 cups (1.5 mL) of juice. (Do not squeeze or force the mixture.) Solids should be discarded. Clean the Dutch oven.

2. Combine the strawberry juice, sugar, and the next 2 ingredients in a Dutch oven, stirring until the sugar dissolves. Over medium-high heat, bring the mixture to a full rolling boil; cook for 1 minute. Fill a heated jar with hot syrup, allowing a 14-inch (.5-cm) headspace. Air bubbles should be removed. Wipe the jar's rim. On the jar, place the lid in the middle. Apply the band and tighten it until it is fingertip-tight. In a boiling-water canner, place the jar. Rep until all of the jars are full. Adjust for altitude and process jars for 10 minutes. Remove jars from heat, remove lids, and set aside for 5 minutes. Remove the jars and set them aside to cool.

NUTRITION

Calories: 30 Kcal	Fat: 8 g
Carbohydrates: 14 g	Protein: 5 g

LONG COOK TRADITIONAL CHERRY PRESERVES

| 🥣 4 Pint Jars | 🍴 Prep Time : 45 Mins | 🕐 Cook Time : 55 Mins |

INGREDIENTS

- ·2 lb cherries
- ·4 cups sugar

DIRECTIONS

1. After washing the cherries under cold running water, drain them. Remove the stems and pits from the cherries over a basin to catch all juices. Set aside the pitted cherries.

2. Combine the cherry juice and sugar in a big stainless-steel or enameled pot. Bring the mixture to a boil, frequently stirring, until all of the sugar has dissolved. Add a dash of water if the juice isn't enough to dissolve the sugar. Place the cherries on top. Bring the cherries to a boil over high heat until they are glossy. Turn off the heat in the pan. After wrapping with plastic wrap, refrigerate for 12 to 18 hours. Bring the mixture to a rolling boil, stirring constantly. Cook fast over high heat, frequently stirring until the liquid almost reaches the gelling point (220°F). Turn off the heat in the pan. Skim the foam if required.

3. Allow a 14-inch headspace in a heated jar partly filled with hot preserves. It's important to get rid of any air bubbles. Wipe the rim of the jar clean. Place the lid in the center of the jar. Tighten the band with your fingertip until it is fingertip-tight. Place the jar in a boiling water canner. Rep the process until all of the jars are full. Process the jars for 10 minutes to adjust for altitude. Take the jars off the heat, take off the lids, and lay them aside for 5 minutes. Take the jars out of the oven and lay them aside to cool.

NUTRITION

Calories: 32 Kcal	Fat: 0 g
Carbohydrates: 21 g	Protein: 0 g

132.

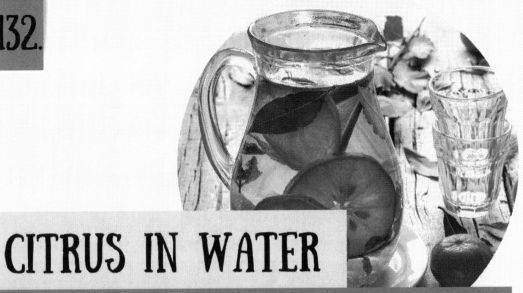

CITRUS IN WATER

 4 Jars | Prep Time : 30 Mins | Cook Time : 60 Mins

INGREDIENTS

·2 to 3 oranges, tangerines, or 1 grapefruit per pint (mixing some grapefruit with oranges or tangerines improves their flavor)

·Lemons or limes can be mixed with other fruit but don't taste well. Can separately.

·Water

DIRECTIONS

1. Warm water is used to wash citrus fruits. Remove all of the skins off the fruit. Remove the fruit's white fibrous substance (albedo). Lemons and limes should be cut into rounds or divided. Bring 1 cup of water to a boil for each pint.

2. Fruit should be placed into jars loosely. Squeezing or compressing is not a good idea. Only about a half-inch of the rim should be left. Pour boiling water over the fruit to fill any gaps and cover it. Remove the bubbles, clean the rims, and set the lids on top. Please make sure the outer peel is clean before peeling it. Using a peeler, remove the whole peel. Divide the fruit into pieces. The fibrous material must be pale and stringy scraped from the inner surface. It has a harsh flavor when canned.

3. Remove as many seeds as possible by cutting off the middle, fibrous area—where the seeds are—with a knife or scissors. Cut grapefruit slices in half if they are too big. Lemons and limes are cut into rounds rather than being sectioned. Fruit slices or rounds should be lightly placed into jars until they reach the shoulders. It's best to leave ½ inch of headspace. The fruit should not be mashed or compressed. It's conceivable that shaking the jars softly may free up some space.

4. If you're using more than one fruit, evenly distribute it throughout the jars. Blood oranges and red grapefruit are used to provide color. Ensure there is enough boiling water to cover all of the fruit before processing. After the bubbles have been eliminated, add extra water if required.

NUTRITION

Calories: 30 Kcal	Fat: 4 g
Carbohydrates: 15 g	Protein: 2 g

PEARS IN JUICE

7 Pint Jars   **Prep Time : 30 Mins** **Cook Time : 60 Mins**

INGREDIENTS

·17 ½ lb pears

COLOR PRESERVATIVE SOLUTION:

·½ cup lemon juice mixed with ½ gallon water or ascorbic acid per label

·1gallon apple juice (not cider)

DIRECTIONS

1. Before cutting into slices, pears should be cleaned and skinned, then sliced lengthwise and cored using a melon baller. Place pear slices in a saucepan with the color preservative solution while the juice is heating.

2. Bring the apple juice to a boil to create it. Drain the peas in a strainer and toss them in with the other ingredients. 5 minutes in the oven. Turn off the heat. Remove air bubbles, clean rims, place lids, and then put sliced pears and juice into heated jars within ½ inch of the top. Pears are peeled using a potato peeler or a paring knife. Cut them lengthwise in half. Scrape out the hard membrane and seeds using a melon baller or a small spoon along the center of the melon.

3. Because pears are irregularly shaped, slices may look better than halves and fit into jars better. When pears are chopped, please put them in the color-preservation solution to avoid discoloring. Because pears are firm, thick fruits, they are cooked for 5 minutes in boiling liquid before being packed into jars.

4. Spoon the pears into jars as soon as possible after completing precooking. Fill each jar with the same quantity of pear slices and liquid. Half-fill jars with hot juice up to the jar rim. Unsweetened white grape juice or pineapple juice is substituted for apple juice.

NUTRITION

Calories: 20 Kcal Fat: 0 g

Carbohydrates: 12 g Protein: 8 g

CHAPTER 8: CHUTNEY AND MARMALADE

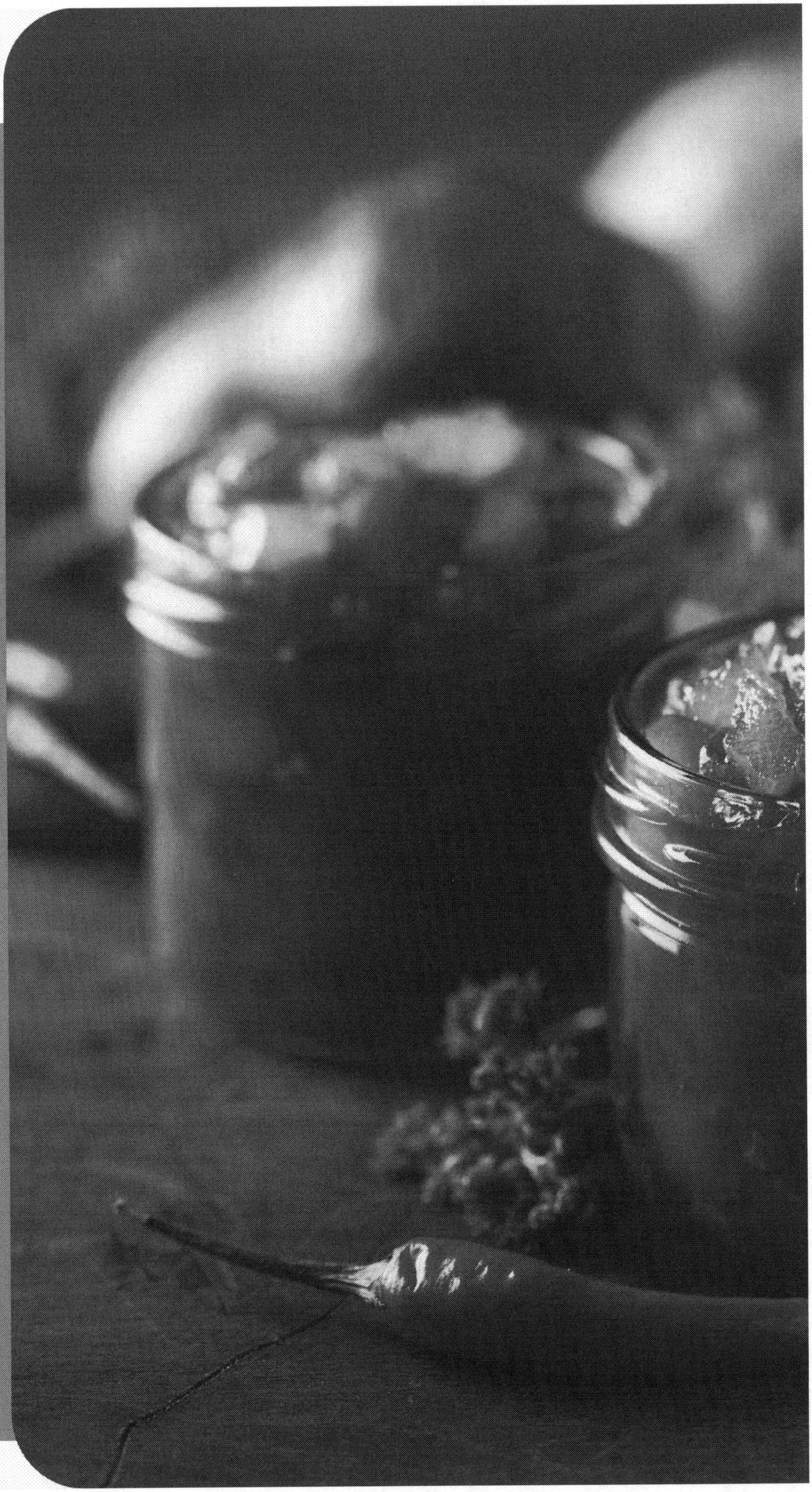

134.

ONION MARMALADE

🥣 **4 Pint Jars** ✖ **Prep Time : 10 Mins** 🕐 **Cook Time : 25 Mins**

INGREDIENTS

- 2 large onions, sliced
- 1 tbsp red wine vinegar
- ⅓ cup red wine
- 1 tsp sugar
- ¼ cup olive oil
- Pinch of salt

DIRECTIONS

1. Warm oil in a small saucepan over medium heat.
2. Add onion and cook for 10 to 15 minutes or until the onion is softened.
3. Add sugar and cook for 5 minutes. Attach wine and cook until wine is reduced.
4. Remove pan from heat. Add vinegar and salt and mix well.
5. Pour marmalade in a clean jar. Secure the jar with a lid and store it in the refrigerator.

NUTRITION

Calories: 159 Kcal	Carbohydrates: 8.6 g	Protein: 0.8 g
Fat: 12.7 g	Sugar: 4.4 g	Cholesterol: 0 mg

TOMATO LEMON MARMALADE

🥣 **9 Pints**   **Prep Time : 10 Mins**   🕐 **Cook Time : 20 Mins**

INGREDIENTS

- 4 cups (4 apples) chopped peeled tart apples
- 5 medium ripe tomatoes
- 6 cups sugar
- 2 medium-seeded and finely chopped lemons
- 8 whole cloves
- 2 ¼ tsp ground ginger

DIRECTIONS

1. Prepare the tomatoes by peeling them, slicing them into quarters, and chopping them.
2. Set chopped tomatoes in a colander to drain before placing them in a Dutch oven.
3. Add the lemons and apples to the Dutch oven, and cook for 15 minutes on moderate heat, stirring often. Stir in ginger and sugar.
4. Place cloves in a cheesecloth bag and tie; add to the mixture.
5. Bring the mixture to a rolling boil, stirring often, and cook until the sugar has melted. Simmer on low for 40 minutes, stirring frequently.
6. Discard the spice bag and ladle the hot marmalade into 9 sterilized hot half-pint jars with a ¼-inch headspace.
7. Remove the air bubbles with a plastic knife, adjust the headspace and wipe the rims.
8. Place the jars into the canner with simmering water, just enough to cover it; bring to a full boil and process it for 10 minutes.
9. Detach the jars and place them on a padded work surface. Let it cool.
10. Enjoy!

NUTRITION

Calories: 142 Kcal	Fiber: 1 g	Carbohydrates: 36 g
Protein: 0 g	Fat: 0 g	

136.

STRAWBERRY AND BLACKBERRY MARMALADE

🥣 **4 Pint Jars**   ✕ **Prep Time : 15 Mins**   🕐 **Cook Time : 5 Mins**

INGREDIENTS

- ·1 lemon
- ·1 ¾ cup fresh strawberries, hulled and crushed
- ·1 cup fresh blackberries, crushed
- ·1 ½ tsp freshly squeezed lemon juice
- ·3 tbsp powdered pectin
- ·3 ½ cups sugar

DIRECTIONS

1. Prepare a hot water bath. Set the jars in it to keep warm. Clean the lids and rings in hot, soapy water, and set them aside.

2. Wash the lemon well with warm, soapy water. Cut half of the rind from the lemon with a sharp knife, removing as much of the pith (white inner membrane) as possible. Slice the rind into thin strips and cut the strips into ¼-inch-long pieces.

3. In a small saucepot set over high heat, combine the lemon rind with enough water to cover. Bring to a boil. Strain and reserve the rind.

4. In a medium saucepot set over high heat, combine the strawberries, blackberries, lemon rind, and lemon juice. Slowly stir in the pectin. Set the mixture to a full, rolling boil.

5. Add the sugar. Return the mixture to a full, rolling boiling over high heat. When the jam cannot be stirred, set a timer for 1 minute and stir constantly. Turn off the heat.

6. With the heat off, stir the marmalade for 1 minute more to ensure even distribution of the rind before filling the jars. Skim off any foam.

7. Ladle the marmalade into the prepared jars, leaving ¼ inch of headspace. Use a nonmetallic utensil to remove any air bubbles. Clean the rims clean and seal them with the lids and rings.

8. Bring the jars into a hot water bath for 10 minutes. Set off the heat and let the jars rest in the water bath for 10 minutes.

9. Carefully detach the jars from the hot water canner. Set aside for 12 hours.

10. Check the lids for proper seals. Detach the rings, wipe the jars, name and date them, and transfer them to a cupboard or pantry. Refrigerate and use within 3 weeks. Properly secure jars will last in the cupboard for 12 months.

NUTRITION

Calories: 49 Kcal	Carbohydrates: 8.7 g	Sugars: 4.9 g
Fat: 0.2 g	Protein: 3.6 g	

GRAPEFRUIT MARMALADE WITH VANILLA

🥣 **4 Pint Jars**   ✕ **Prep Time : 25 Mins**   🕐 **Cook Time : 60 Mins**

INGREDIENTS

- 3 grape fruits
- 3 cups sugar
- 1 whole vanilla bean

DIRECTIONS

1. Prepare a hot water bath. Set the jars in it to keep warm. Clean the lids and rings in hot, soapy water, and set them aside.
2. Wash the grapefruits well with warm, soapy water. With a sharp knife, remove the grapefruit rind. Stack into piles and slice into strips. Mince the strips.
3. Mix the minced rind with enough water to cover in a small saucepan over medium heat. Bring to a simmer. Cook for 20 minutes or until tender.
4. While the rind cooks, remove any remaining pith from the grapefruit with your hands or a knife. Working on a bowl to catch the juice, slice along the membranes, removing each grapefruit segment individually. Attach the segments to the bowl with the juice. When finished, squeeze the remaining membranes over the bowl to collect any additional juice. Discard the membranes and seeds.
5. Strain the rind, reserving 2 cups of the cooking liquid.
6. In a medium saucepot set over medium-high heat, combine the reserved cooking liquid, sugar, rind, and grapefruit segments in their juices. Bring to a full, rolling boil. Cook for 35 to 45 minutes until it reaches 220°F (104°C), measured with a candy thermometer.
7. Add the vanilla bean seeds. Turn off the heat. Use the plate test to determine if the marmalade sets. If not, return the pot to the burner and cook in five-minute increments until it sets to your liking.
8. With the heat off, stir the marmalade for 1 minute to evenly distribute the rind. Skim off any foam.
9. Ladle the marmalade into the prepared jars, leaving ¼ inch of headspace. Use a nonmetallic utensil to remove any air bubbles. Wipe the rims clean and seal them using the lids and rings.
10. Set the jars in a hot water bath for 10 minutes. Set off the heat and bring the jars to rest in the water bath for 10 minutes.
11. Carefully detach the jars from the hot water canner. Set aside to cool for 12 hours.
12. Check the lids for proper seals. Detach the rings, clean the jars, label and date them, and transfer them to a cupboard or pantry.
13. Use within 3 weeks.

NUTRITION

Calories: 149	Carbohydrates: 37.7 g
Fat: 0.4 g	Protein: 1.3 g

138.

ORANGE MARMALADE

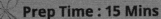 🥣 2 Pint Jars ✂️ Prep Time : 15 Mins Cook Time : 15 Mins

INGREDIENTS

- ½ cup water
- 4 medium navel oranges, peeled and cut into small pieces
- 2 cups sugar

DIRECTIONS

1. Add the orange pieces to a blender or food processor. Blend well.

2. In a deep saucepan, combine the orange mixture, water, and sugar.

3. Set the mixture till the thermometer reads 220°F; cook for about 12 to 15 minutes over medium heat until firm and thick. Stir continually to prevent scorching.

4. Spill the hot mixture into pre-sterilized jars directly or with a jar funnel. Keep a headspace of ¼ inch from the jar top.

5. To detach tiny air bubbles, insert a nonmetallic spatula and stir the mixture gently.

6. Clean the sealing edges with a damp cloth. Secure the jars with the lids and adjust the bands/rings to seal and prevent leakage.

7. Set the jars in a cool, dry, and dark place. Allow them to cool down completely.

Store in your refrigerator and use within 10 days

NUTRITION

Calories: 4 Kcal	Fat: 0 g	Sodium: 727 mg
Carbohydrates: 1 g	Protein: 1 g	

SUPER TANGY MARMALADE

3 Pint Jars **Prep Time : 5 Mins** **Cook Time : 30 Mins**

INGREDIENTS

· 3 ½ cups white granulated sugar

· 1 cup limes, unpeeled and thinly sliced

· 1 cup lemons, unpeeled and thinly sliced

3 cups water

DIRECTIONS

1. Mix the citrus slices and water in a deep saucepan or cooking pot.

2. Boil the mixture, and simmer for a few minutes over low heat.

3. Mix in the sugar.

4. Boil the mixture and cook for about 25 to 30 minutes over medium heat until firm and thick. Swirl continually to prevent scorching.

5. Spill the hot mixture into pre-sterilized jars directly or with a jar funnel. Keep a headspace of ¼ inch from the jar top.

6. To detach tiny air bubbles, insert a nonmetallic spatula and stir the mixture gently.

7. Clean the sealing edges with a damp cloth. Secure the jars with the lids and adjust the bands/rings to seal and prevent leakage.

8. Set the jars in a cool, dry, and dark place. Allow them to cool down completely.

9. Store in your refrigerator and use within 10 days.

NUTRITION

Calories: 37   Carbohydrates: 7.4 g   Sugar: 1.3 g

Protein: 1.9 g   Fat: 0.8 g

LEMON MARMALADE

 6 Pint Jars   Prep Time : 40 Mins 🕐 Cook Time : 10 Mins

INGREDIENTS

- 3 medium lemons
- 1 medium grapefruit
- 4 cups water
- 1 package of powdered fruit pectin
- 4 cups sugar

DIRECTIONS

1. Peel rind from lemons and grapefruit and cut into 1-inch long strips.

2. In a Dutch oven, combine citrus peel and water. Bring to a boil. Reduce heat, then simmer, covered, for 5 to 7 minutes, until peel softened. Remove from heat, then set it aside.

3. Trim the white pith from reserved grapefruit and lemons. Cut grapefruit and lemons in segments, discarding seeds and membranes.

4. Chop pulp, reserving juices, and then stir into reserved peel mixture.

5. Add pectin. Bring to a boil, stirring constantly.

6. Stir in sugar while letting it boil, stirring for 1 minute.

7. Remove from heat and skim off the foam.

8. Scoop hot mixture into 6 hot sterilized half-pint jars, leaving ¼-inch headspace. Remove the air bubbles and, if necessary, adjust the headspace by adding a hot mixture. Wipe rims carefully. Place the tops on jars and screw on bands until fingertip tight.

9. Place jars in a canner with boiling water, ensuring they are completely covered with water. Let boil for 10 minutes. Remove jars and cool.

NUTRITION

Calories: 67 Kcal	Total Carbohydrates: 17 g
Total Fat: 0 g	Protein: 0 g

PEAR MARMALADE

🥣 12 Pint Jars   ✂ Prep Time : 10 Mins   🕐 Cook Time : 10 Mins

INGREDIENTS

- 4 medium-ripe pears, peeled and quartered
- 5 ½ cups sugar
- 1.75 oz pectin
- 1 tbsp orange zest, grated
- 2 tbsp lemon juice
- ½ cup orange juice
- 8 oz crushed pineapple

DIRECTIONS

1. Add pears into the food processor and process until pureed.
2. Add pear puree, pectin, orange zest, lemon juice, orange juice, and pineapple into the saucepan and bring to a boil over high heat. Stir constantly.
3. Add sugar and stir well and boil for 1 minute. Stir constantly.
4. Remove the pot from heat and let it cool completely.
5. Pour marmalade in a clean jar. Secure the jar with a lid and store it in the refrigerator.

NUTRITION

Calories: 393 Kcal   Total Carbohydrates: 40.1 g

Total Fat: 0.1 g   Proteins: 0.4 g

142.

PINEAPPLE MARMALADE

 8 Pint Jars   Prep Time : 10 Mins   🕐 Cook Time : 45 Mins

INGREDIENTS

- 3 ½ cups shredded pineapple flesh
- ½ lemon, sliced
- 4 ½ cups sugar
- 4 cups water

DIRECTIONS

1. Add pineapple, lemon, and water to a saucepan. Cover and let sit overnight.
2. Boil the pineapple mixture for 20 minutes.
3. Attach sugar and stir until sugar is dissolved.
4. Boil the pineapple mixture for 25 minutes.
5. Remove the saucepan from the heat.
6. Pour the marmalade into the clean jars.
7. Seal jar with lids. Name and store in a cool and dry place.

NUTRITION

Calories: 202 Kcal	Total Carbohydrates: 53 g
Total Fat: 0 g	Protein: 0.2 g

GREEN TOMATO CHUTNEY

🥣 3 Pint Jars   Prep Time : 15 Mins   🕐 Cook Time : 15 Mins

INGREDIENTS

·2 ½ lb firm green tomatoes, chopped

·1 ¼ cup brown sugar, packed

·1 cup red onion, chopped

·1 cup golden raisins

·1 cup cider vinegar

·2 tbsp candied ginger, minced

·1 tbsp mustard seeds

·1 tsp chili pepper flakes

·1 tsp fennel seeds

·1 tsp salt

·½ tsp ground allspice

· tsp ground cloves

·1 cinnamon stick

·Pinch of ground nutmeg

DIRECTIONS

1.   Place all of the ingredients in a 4-quart pot. Bring to a boil and then reduce to a simmer. Cover the pot and cook for 45 minutes.

2. Spoon the chutney into sterilized jars, filling them to ¼ inch from the rim. Wipe the rims clean and place lids on the jars. Process for 15 minutes in a boiling water bath.

NUTRITION

Calories: 18.2 Kcal	Fat: 0 g	Protein: 0 g
Cholesterol: 0 mg	Carbohydrates: 6 g	Sugar: 79.17 g

144.

JERI'S DILL RELISH

 4 Pint Jars   Prep Time : 15 Mins   Cook Time : 25 Mins

INGREDIENTS

- 8 cups cucumbers, chopped
- 2 green sweet peppers
- 1 yellow or orange sweet pepper
- 1 red sweet pepper
- 1 ½ cup onion
- ½ cup salt
- 5 cups white vinegar
- 1 tsp ground mustard
- 3 large heads of fresh dill or 3 tbsp dry dill seed

DIRECTIONS

1. Remove stems and blossom end of cukes, seeds, and ribs of peppers, and then run all vegetables through a meat grinder with a coarse blade.
2. Place in a large pan and sprinkle salt over vegetables.
3. Add cold water to cover and stir to distribute the salt. Let stand for 3 hours. Drain well.
4. In a large pot, add vinegar, mustard, and dill. Bring to a boil and simmer for about 10 minutes.
5. Remove dill heads.
6. Add ground vegetables and heat just to a boil, stirring to distribute heat.
7. Package the hot relish into sterilized, hot jars or pints, allowing ½ inch of headspace. Wipe the jar's rim; set a warm lid in place and tighten. Place in a bath canner with boiling water and process for 15 minutes.

NUTRITION

Calories: 0 Kcal	Fat: 0 g	Protein: 0 g
Cholesterol: 0 mg	Carbohydrates: 0 g	Sugars: 7.39 g

RHUBARB CHERRY CHUTNEY

🥣 6 Pint Jars   ✂ Prep Time : 15 Mins   🕐 Cook Time : 35 Mins

INGREDIENTS

- ·2 lb chopped fresh rhubarb
- ·2 cups chopped cherries
- ·1 chopped apple
- ·1 chopped red onion
- ·1 chopped celery rib
- ·3 minced garlic cloves
- ·1 tbsp chopped crystallized ginger
- ·2 cups brown sugar
- ·1 cup red wine vinegar
- ·¾ tsp ground cinnamon
- ·½ tsp ground coriander
- ·¼ tsp ground cloves

DIRECTIONS

1. In a 6-quart stockpot, combine all ingredients and allow to boil.
2. Simmer for 30 minutes while uncovered.
3. Transfer to covered containers. If freezing, use freezer-safe containers and fill to within ½ inch of the tops.
4. Freeze for up to 12 months or refrigerate for up to 3 weeks. Before serving, thaw the frozen salsa in the refrigerator.

NUTRITION

Calories: 102 Kcal	Fat: 0 g	Protein: 0 g
Carbohydrates: 27 g	Protein: 0 g	Sugar: 79.17 g

146.

GARLICKY LIME CHUTNEY

3 Pint Jars   **Prep Time : 10 Mins**   **Cook Time : 25 Mins**

INGREDIENTS

· 12 limes, scrubbed and cut into ½-inch dice

· 12 garlic cloves thinly sliced lengthwise

· 1 (4-inch) piece of fresh ginger, peeled and thinly sliced

· 8 green chili peppers (jalapeños or Serrano's), stemmed, seeded, and thinly sliced

· 1 tbsp chili powder

· 1 cup distilled white vinegar

· ¾ cup sugar

DIRECTIONS

1. Prepare a hot water bath. Bring the jars in it to keep warm. Clean the lids and rings in hot, soapy water, and set them aside.

2. In a medium saucepan, combine the limes, garlic, ginger, chiles, and chili powder, stir well, and bring to a simmer.

3. Add the vinegar and sugar, return to a simmer, and cook, occasionally stirring, until the limes are tender, and the mixture is thick to the mound when dropped from a spoon, about 70 minutes. Remove from the heat.

4. Ladle the chutney into the prepared jars, leaving ¼ inch of headspace. Use a nonmetallic utensil to free any air bubbles. Clean the rims and seal with the lids and rings.

5. Set the jars in a hot water bath for 20 minutes. Set off the heat and let the jars rest in the water bath.

6. Carefully detach the jars from the hot water canner. Set aside to cool for 12 hours.

7. Check the lids for proper seals. Remove the rings, wipe the jars, label and date them, and transfer them to a cupboard or pantry.

8. For the best flavor, allow the chutney to rest for 3 days before serving. Set in the refrigerator any jars that don't seal properly and use them within 6 weeks. Properly secure jars will last in the cupboard for 12 months. Once opened, refrigerate and consume within 6 weeks.

NUTRITION

Calories: 58 Kcal   Carbohydrates: 12 g

Fat: 1 g   Protein: 0 g

CILANTRO CHUTNEY

🥣 5 Pint Jars   ✂ Prep Time : 45 Mins   🕐 Cook Time : 10 Mins

INGREDIENTS

·½ cup yogurt (this can be omitted or replaced with a vegan-based version of yogurt)

·3 tbsp lemon juice

·1 bunch of cilantro with stems removed (small branches can be left intact)

·1 cup packed Mint leaves

·2 tsp ginger, sliced

·½ tsp sea salt

·1 garlic clove

·1 medium-sized jalapeño, sliced finely

·½ tsp sugar

DIRECTIONS

1.   Merge all the ingredients above in a blender with 1 tbsp of water.

2.   Taste and add more spice as needed, pour it into a sterilized jar, and store it in the refrigerator. You can add coconut or soy-based yogurt if you want to substitute the yogurt for a non-dairy alternative. Tofu is another option to consider.

3.   If you wish to preserve it for a longer period, omit the yogurt entirely and store the chutney in a jar for up to one month in your refrigerator.

NUTRITION

Calories: 88 Kcal	Fat: 0 g
Carbohydrates: 22 g	Protein: 1 g

148.

INDIAN APPLE CHUTNEY

🥣 6 Pint Jars ✂ Prep Time : 15 Mins ⏰ Cook Time : 20 Mins

INGREDIENTS

·2 lb apples (medium in size)

·1 cup diced onions (finely diced)

·2 tsp allspice

·2 tbsp ginger, ground or fresh

·7 cups or 2 lb raisins

·1 cup red bell pepper, chopped finely

·3 tbsp mustard seeds

·2 tsp curry powder

·2 tsp pickling salt

·1 garlic clove, crushed

·2 hot peppers, seeds removed and diced finely

·4 cups malt vinegar

·4 cups brown sugar (or less, if you prefer less sugar)

DIRECTIONS

1. Prepare, wash, and scrub the apples. Then peel, core, and slice. Place the apples in a large cooking pot and cover them with water. Wash and slice the onions, remove all the skin, and add to the cooking pot.

2. Repeat the same process with the peppers and add them to the pot with the onions and apples.

3. Pour the remaining ingredients into the cooking pot, including the malt vinegar, and bring the contents to a boil. Once this point is reached, cook for about 2 minutes, then reduce to a simmer and stir often.

4. Continue this process until the apples are tender, which can take up to 1 hour. Place the mixture into sterilized jars and adjust for one inch of space at the top.

5. Clean down the jars' rims before scooping the chutney's contents into the jars. Place the lids on tightly and process in a water bath canner for 10 to 11 minutes.

6. Allow the jars to cool on a wire rack or cloth overnight, then store them in a pantry or fruit cellar for up to one month.

NUTRITION

Calories: 47 Kcal	Carbohydrates: 11.1 g
Fat: 0 g	Protein: 0 g

PLUM TOMATO CHUTNEY

🥣 4 Pint Jars	✂ Prep Time : 15 Mins	🕐 Cook Time : 15 Mins

INGREDIENTS

- ·4 tomatoes, chopped
- ·6 plums, seeded and chopped
- ·2 green chilies, chopped
- ·4 tbsp fresh ginger, grated
- ·1 tsp lemon zest
- ·1 lemon juice
- ·2 bay leaves
- ·Pinch of salt
- ·½ cup + 2 tbsp brown sugar
- ·2 tsp vinegar
- ·Pinch black pepper
- ·4 tsp vegetable oil

DIRECTIONS

Heat the oil in a deep saucepan.

1.   Add the bay leaves, ginger, and green chilies, and stir. Add the tomatoes and plums.

2.   Add the salt, zest, lemon juice, and vinegar. Stir in the sugar and pepper, cover, and cook for 3 minutes.

3.   Spoon the chutney into sterilized jars, leaving a ½–inch headspace.

4.   Wipe the edge of the jar rim clean and add the lid. Process these in a boiling water bath for 10 minutes.

NUTRITION

Calories: 70	Carbohydrates: 31 g
Fat: 0 g	Protein: 1 g

191

150.

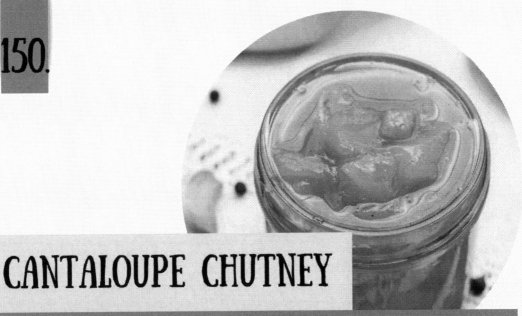

CANTALOUPE CHUTNEY

🥣 **3 Pint Jars** ✂ **Prep Time : 15 Mins** **Cook Time : 90 Mins**

INGREDIENTS

- 3 medium cantaloupes
- 1 lb dried apricots
- 1 fresh hot chili
- 2 cups raisins
- 1 tsp ground cloves
- 1 tsp ground nutmeg
- 2 tbsp salt
- 2 tbsp mustard seed
- ¼ cup fresh ginger, chopped
- 3 garlic cloves
- 4 ½ cups apple cider vinegar
- 2 ¼ cups brown sugar
- 4 onions
- ½ cup orange juice
- 2 tbsp orange zest

DIRECTIONS

1. Thinly slice the apricots and put them into a large bowl.
2. Chop the ginger and garlic thinly, and add to the dish.
3. Stir in chili, seed, and dice, and add to the pot.
4. Add raisins, cloves, cinnamon, nutmeg, and mustard seeds.
5. Mix and set aside.
6. Combine the vinegar and sugar in a non-reactive pot or kettle; bring to a boil over medium heat.
7. Add mixture to the pot in a bowl and return to a moderate simmer.
8. Keep simmer for 45 minutes. Do not deck the pot.
9. Meanwhile, onions are chopped and placed in a bowl.
10. Cantaloupes fifth, peel, and seed.
11. Split the fruit into half-inch cubes.
12. Add onions.
13. In a cup, add orange juice and zest; mix well.
14. Once the vinegar mixture has ended 45 minutes of cooking time, add the cantaloupe mixture to the bowl, bring it back to a cooler, and start cooking for another 45 minutes or until thickened at the simmer.
15. Pour into hot glasses, clean the rims, and screw the lids and rings together.
16. Boiling water bath process: pints and quarts 10 minutes in, both.

NUTRITION

Calories: 54 Kcal	Fat: 0 g	Protein: 1 g
Cholesterol: 0 mg	Carbohydrates: 14 g	Sugar: 139.47 g

MANGO CHUTNEY

🥣 **4 Pint Jars**   ✂️ **Prep Time : 15 Mins**   🕐 **Cook Time : 45 Mins**

INGREDIENTS

- 6 cups sliced green mangos
- ½ lb fresh ginger
- 3 ½ cups currants
- 8 cups sugar
- 2 cups vinegar
- 3 cups ground cayenne pepper
- 1 cup salt

DIRECTIONS

1. Peel the ginger and halve it.
2. Slice one half of the ginger into thin slices; chop the other half of the ginger roughly.
3. Grind the sliced ginger with half of the currants using a blender until well combined. Place all in a saucepan, except the mangoes.
4. Cook over medium heat for 15 minutes.
5. Meanwhile, to set 6 cups, cut, halve, pit, and slice the green mangos.
6. After 15 minutes of cooking, attach the mangos and parboil for another 30 minutes until the mangos are tender.
7. Pour into shot glasses, clean the rims, and screw the lids and rings together.
8. Use the boiling water bath process: pints and quarts for 10 minutes in both
9. Serve warm.

NUTRITION

Calories: 37 Kcal	Calories: 37 Kcal
Total Fat: 0 g	Total Fat: 0 g

152.

ORANGE CRANBERRY CHUTNEY

🥣 3 Pint Jars Prep Time : 15 Mins Cook Time : 20 Mins

INGREDIENTS

- 2 cups chopped white onion
- 2 cups white vinegar
- 3 cinnamon sticks
- 1 ½ cup sugar
- 4 tbsp grated ginger
- 24 oz fresh cranberries
- 2 cups golden raisins
- 1 cup orange juice

DIRECTIONS

1. After thoroughly rinsing the cranberries, put them in a Dutch oven (large).
2. Add other ingredients and toss to combine.
3. Boil the mixture over high heat.
4. Simmer for 15 minutes or until you're sure the cranberries are tenderized. Make sure to stir to avoid scorching frequently.
5. Once the chutney is done, discard the cinnamon sticks. Pour the chutney into clean and hot Mason jars (half-pint), making sure to leave half an inch of headspace in each.
6. Get rid of air bubbles in the jars before fitting their rims with the lids. Place in the pressure canner.
7. Process for 10 minutes.

NUTRITION

Calories: 72.4 Kcal Total Carbohydrates: 18.2 g

Total Fat: 0.1 g Protein: 0.3 g

CHAPTER 9: PICKLES AND RELISH

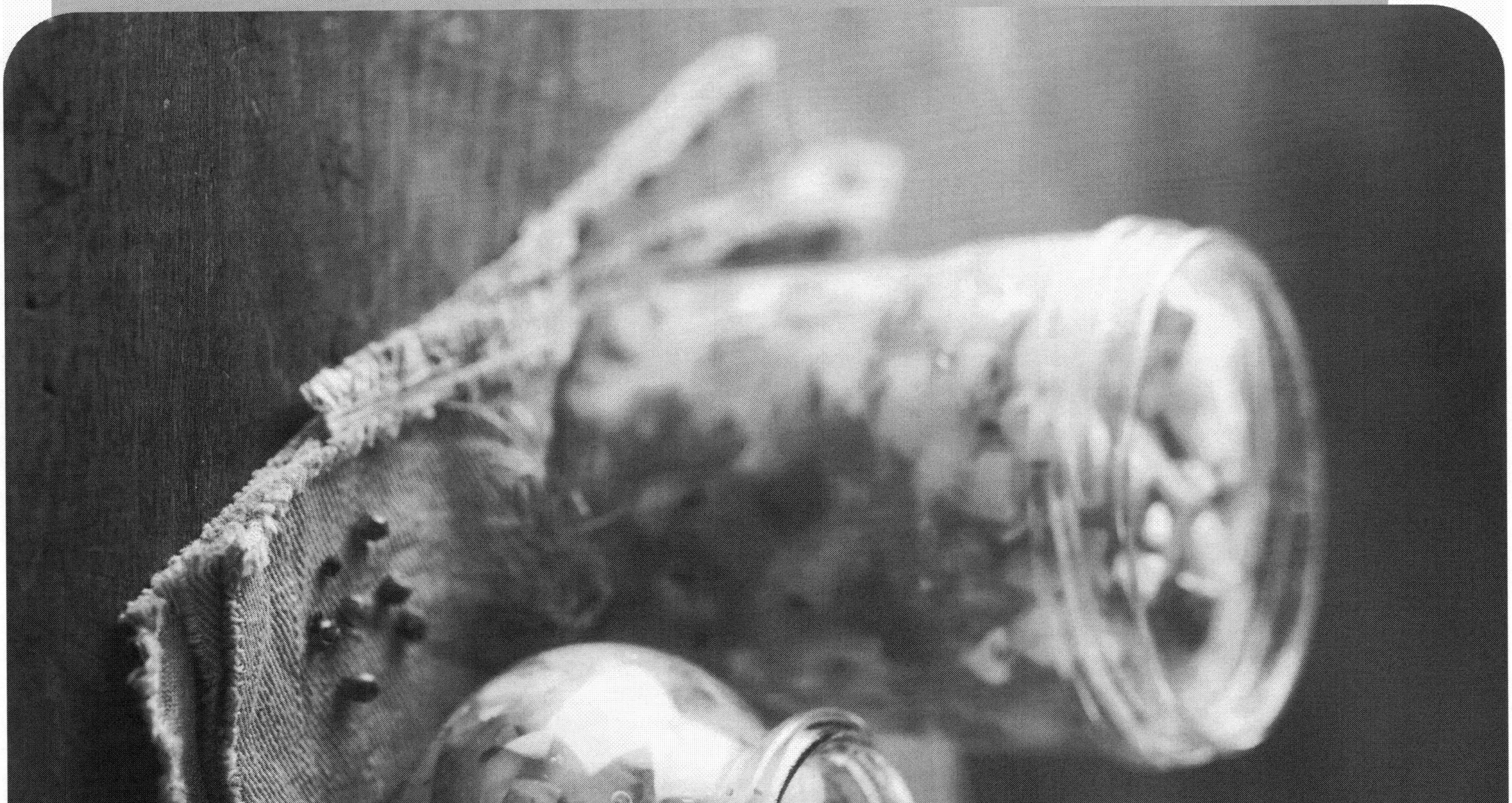

153.

PICKLED BEETS

🥣 6   **Prep Time : 5 Mins**   **Cook Time : 10 Mins**

INGREDIENTS

- 2 cups water
- 2 cups white vinegar
- 2 cups sugar
- 1 tsp salt
- 3 ½ lb dark red beets
- 1 to 2 yellow or white onions

DIRECTIONS

1. Wash the beets, place them in a large kettle, and cover them with water. Bring to a boil and let them cook until tender. You know they're ready when you can insert the knife in with just a bit of resistance. Test and remove individually.

2. After they're cooked, drain, let cool and use a knife to remove the skin. On the stove, combine the water, white vinegar, sugar, and salt, and bring to a simmer.

3. Start up a large kettle with water on high heat to process your jars. Slice up the onions and beets and put them in the jar.

4. Make sure there are onions on top of the beets. Give it about ½-inch of headspace. Bring the brine to a hard boil and fill the jars, maintain headspace.

5. Process for 10 minutes. Once done, remove the jars from the kettle and let them cool completely and naturally.

NUTRITION

Calories: 128 Kcal	Protein: 1.9 g
Carbohydrates: 30.3 g	Fat: 0.2 g

PICKLED CURRY CAULIFLOWER

🍲 6   ✂️ **Prep Time : 5 Mins**   🕐 **Cook Time : 15 Mins**

INGREDIENTS

- 1 ½ tbsp canning salt
- 4 cups vinegar
- 3 cups water
- 3 tsp cumin seeds
- 3 tsp turmeric
- 3 tsp curry powder
- 5 lb cauliflower
- 6 Serrano peppers

DIRECTIONS

1. With a 4-quart kettle, combine the water, salt, and vinegar. Simmer over medium-low heat and whisk to help dissolve the salt. Keep hot until ready to use.

2. Pack jars with cauliflower. Add ½ tsp cumin seeds, turmeric, curry flower, and 1 Serrano pepper into each jar.

3. Pour hot brine into the jars, leaving ½ inch headspace. Process for 12 minutes. Remove from water, and let cool for 12 hours.

NUTRITION

Calories: 34 Kcal   Protein: 2 g

Carbohydrates: 5.3 g   Fat: 0.4 g

155.

ZUCCHINI PICKLE

🥣 44　　✂ **Prep Time : 5 Mins**　　🕐 **Cook Time : 10 Mins**

INGREDIENTS

· 11 cups zucchini (sliced thinly)
· cup canning salt
· 4 ½ cups white vinegar
· 3 cups sugar
· 1 ½ tsp turmeric (ground)
· 1 onion (halved, sliced thin)
· 1 tbsp mustard seeds

DIRECTIONS

1.　Clean and sterilize the jars. Toss the onion, zucchini, and salt together in a mixing dish. Cover with water and place in the refrigerator for 2 hours. Drain and rinse.

2.　In a saucepan, combine the other ingredients and bring to a boil, constantly stirring to dissolve the sugar. Simmer for 5 minutes on low heat before adding the onion and zucchini. Bring to a boil once more, stirring occasionally. Cook for 5 minutes on low heat.

3.　Fill the sterilized jars halfway with the heated mixture, allowing a half-inch headspace. Remove any air bubbles and thoroughly clean them. Apply the bands and cover the jars with the lids, ensuring they are tight. Submerge the jars in a hot water canner for 10 minutes to finish the procedure.

4.　Remove the jars from the oven, let them cool, and then label them.

NUTRITION

Calories: 12 Kcal	Carbohydrates: 3 g
Fat: 0 g	Protein: 0 g

MUSHROOM PICKLE

 64   **Prep Time : 5 Mins**   **Cook Time : 15 Mins**

INGREDIENTS

- ·5 lb mushrooms
- ·2 cups vinegar
- ·1 ½ cup canola oil
- ·2 onions
- ·2 tbsp salt
- ·¼ tsp tarragon
- ·3 garlic cloves
- ·¼ cup sugar
- ·½ tsp pepper

DIRECTIONS

1. Clean and sterilize the jars. Bring all of the ingredients to a boil in a saucepan. Cook for 10 minutes on low heat. Fill the sterilized jars halfway with the heated mixture, allowing a half-inch headspace. Remove any air bubbles and thoroughly clean them. Apply the bands and cover the jars with the lids, ensuring they are tight. Submerge the jars in a hot water canner for 20 minutes to complete the procedure.

2. Remove the jars from the oven, let them cool, and then label them.

NUTRITION

Calories: 18 Kcal   Carbohydrates: 2 g

Fat: 1 g   Protein: 1 g

157.

SWEET PEPPER PICKLE

 54   **Prep Time : 15 Mins**   **Cook Time : 20 Mins**

INGREDIENTS

- ·5 sweet red peppers
- ·1 onion (halved, sliced thinly)
- ·2 ½ cups water
- ·8 banana peppers (seeded, cut into strips)
- ·1 ¼ cup sugar
- ·2 tsp canning salt
- ·4 tsp canola oil
- ·8 garlic cloves (peeled)
- ·2 ½ cups white vinegar

DIRECTIONS

1.   Fill the jars with red peppers, bananas, and oil after sterilizing them. Bring the sugar, salt, and water to a boil in a saucepan. Fill the sterilized jars halfway with the heated mixture, allowing a half-inch headspace. Remove any air bubbles and thoroughly clean them. Apply the bands and cover the jar, ensuring they are tight. Place the jars in a hot water canner and process for 15 minutes.

2.   Remove the jars from the oven, let them cool, and label them.

3.   Store them and enjoy.

NUTRITION

Calories: 13 Kcal   Carbohydrates: 3 g

Fat: 0 g   Protein: 0 g

OKRA PICKLE

🥣 64   ✕ **Prep Time : 5 Mins**   🕐 **Cook Time : 15 Mins**

INGREDIENTS

- 2 lb okra
- 7 garlic cloves
- 7 hot peppers
- 7 tbsp salt
- 3 ½ tsp dill seeds
- 3 ½ tsp mustard seeds

PICKLING MIX:

- 3 ½ cups water
- ½ cup lemon juice
- 4 cups white vinegar

DIRECTIONS

1. Clean and sterilize the jars. Divide the hot peppers, garlic cloves, salt, dill seeds, mustard seeds, pickling mix, and okra between the jars. Fill the sterilized jars halfway with the heated mixture, allowing a half-inch headspace. Remove any air bubbles and thoroughly clean them apply the bands and cover the jars with the lids, ensuring they are tight. Submerge the jars in a hot water canner for 10 minutes to finish the procedure.

2. Remove the jars from the oven, let them cool, and then label them.

NUTRITION

Calories: 19 Kcal	Carbohydrates: 3.7 g
Fat: 0.1 g	Protein: 0.9 g

159.

EGGPLANT PICKLE

 28   **Prep Time : 10 Mins**   **Cook Time : 20 Mins**

INGREDIENTS

- 2 ¼ lb eggplant (peeled, cubed)
- 3 cups white wine vinegar
- ¼ cup basil
- 2 tbsp garlic (minced)
- 2 tbsp salt

DIRECTIONS

1. Clean and sterilize the jars. In a saucepan, bring the vinegar to a boil, add a quarter of the eggplant and cook for 2 minutes. Transfer the eggplant to a bowl using a spoon filter, and continue with the remaining eggplant. Combine the eggplant, basil, salt, and garlic in a mixing bowl.

2. Fill the sterilized jars halfway with the heated mixture, allowing a half-inch headspace. Remove any air bubbles and thoroughly clean them. Apply the bands and cover the jars with the lids, ensuring they are tight. Submerge the jars in a hot water canner for 10 minutes to finish the procedure.

3. Remove the jars from the oven, let them cool, and then label them.

NUTRITION

Calories: 36 Kcal   Carbohydrates: 6 g

Fat: 0.2 g   Protein: 0.9 g

SPICED DILL PICKLE

🥣 28　　✂️ Prep Time : 5 Mins　　🕐 Cook Time : 20 Mins

INGREDIENTS

- ·8 lb Kirby cucumbers
- ·4 cups water
- ·7 tsp dill seeds
- ·4 cups white vinegar
- ·3 tbsp spice
- ·¾ cup white sugar
- ·7 bay leaves
- ·7 garlic cloves
- ·3 ¾ tsp red pepper flakes

DIRECTIONS

1. After sterilizing them, disperse the bay leaves, red pepper flakes, dill seeds, and garlic between the jars. Fill each jar halfway with cucumbers. In a saucepan, combine the water, vinegar, salt, sugar, and pickling spice and bring to a boil, then cover and simmer for 15 minutes. Fill the sterilized jars halfway with the heated mixture, allowing a half-inch headspace. Remove any air bubbles and thoroughly clean them. Apply the bands and cover the jars with the lids, ensuring they are tight. Place the jars in a hot water canner and process for 15 minutes.

2. Remove the jars from the oven, let them cool, and then label them.

NUTRITION

Calories: 33 Kcal　　Carbohydrates: 6.7 g

Fat: 0.4 g　　Protein: 1 g

161.

JALAPEÑO PICKLE

 40   **Prep Time : 10 Mins**   **Cook Time : 20 Mins**

INGREDIENTS

- 2 ¾ lb jalapeños
- 3 garlic cloves
- 2 cups water
- 6 cups vinegar

DIRECTIONS

1. Fill the jars with the jalapenos after sterilizing them. In a saucepan, combine the water, vinegar, and garlic, bring to a boil, reduce to low heat and simmer for 5 minutes. Garlic should be discarded. Fill the sterilized jars halfway with the heated mixture, allowing a half-inch headspace. Remove any air bubbles and thoroughly clean them. Apply the bands and cover the jars with the lids, ensuring they are tight. Submerge the jars in a hot water canner for 10 minutes to finish the procedure.

2. Remove the jars from the oven, let them cool, and then label them.

NUTRITION

Calories: 9 Kcal   Carbohydrates: 1.8 g

Fat: 0.2 g   Protein: 0.4 g

CAULIFLOWER & PEPPER PICKLE

32   Prep Time : 15 Mins   Cook Time : 10 Mins

INGREDIENTS

- 3 lb cauliflower
- 10 oz pearl onion
- 8 bay leaves
- 4 tbsp salt
- 14 oz sweet red peppers
- 2 cups water
- 5 oz banana peppers
- 2 tbsp coriander seeds
- 4 tbsp mustard
- 10 oz sugar
- 5 cups apple vinegar
- 8 cloves
- 8 garlic cloves

DIRECTIONS

1. Divide the garlic, cloves, and bay leaves among jars. In a saucepan, combine the water, vinegar, sugar, salt, and mustard seeds and bring to a boil; reduce to low heat and simmer for 3 minutes. Fill the jars with vegetables. Fill the jars halfway with the heated mixture, allowing a half-inch headspace. Remove any air bubbles and thoroughly clean them. Apply the bands and cover the jars with the lids, ensuring they are tight. Place the jars in a hot water canner and process for 15 minutes.

2. Remove the jars from the oven, let them cool, and then label them.

NUTRITION

Calories: 63 Kcal   Carbohydrates: 12.6 g

Fat: 0.7 g   Protein: 2 g

163.

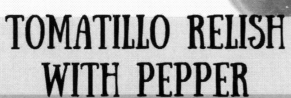

TOMATILLO RELISH WITH PEPPER

🥣 **6 Pint Jars**   ✈ **Prep Time : 15 Mins**   🕐 **Cook Time : 25 Mins**

INGREDIENTS

·12 cups chopped tomatillos

·3 cups finely chopped jicama

·3 cups chopped onion

·6 cups chopped plum-type tomatoes

·1 ½ cup chopped green bell pepper

·1 ½ cup chopped red bell pepper

·1 ½ cup chopped yellow bell pepper

·1 cup canning salt

·2 qt water

·6 tbsp whole mixed pickling spice

·1 tbsp crushed red pepper flakes, optional

·6 cups sugar

·6 ½ cups cider vinegar (5%)

DIRECTIONS

1. Detach husks from tomatillos and wash well.
2.   Skin jicama and onion. Clean all vegetables well before trimming and chopping. Set chopped tomatillos, jicama, onion, tomatoes, and all bell peppers in a 4-quart saucepot.
3.   Set canning salt in water. Spill over-prepared vegetables.
4.   Warmth to boiling; parboil for 5 minutes. Drain thoroughly for about 15 to 20 minutes.
5.   Set pickling spice and optional red pepper flakes on a clean, double-layer, 6-inch-square piece of 100% cotton cheesecloth.
6.   Set corners together and tie them with a clean string. (Or use a purchased muslin spice bag.)
7.   Merge sugar, vinegar, and spices in a saucepan; set to a boil.
8.   Attached drained vegetables. Return to boil; set heat and simmer, uncovered, for 30 minutes. Remove the spice bag.
9.   Set hot relish mixture into hot pint jars, giving ½ inch headspace.
10. Detach air bubbles and adjust headspace if needed.
11. Clean the rims of jars with a dampened, clean paper towel. Adjust lids and process.

NUTRITION

Calories: 88 Kcal	Fibero g	Carbohydrates: 23 g
Protein: 0 g	Fat: 0 g	

SPICY CORN RELISH

🥣 **4 Pint Jars**   ✂️ **Prep Time : 15 Mins**   🕐 **Cook Time : 35 Mins**

INGREDIENTS

·Fresh corn on the cob (about 18)

·2 cups red bell peppers, sliced

·1 ½ cup diced green peppers

·½ cup jalapeno, chopped finely, optional

·2 to 3 garlic cloves crushed

·2 tbsp sea salt

·4 tsp dried mustard powder

·⅔ cup brown sugar

·4 cups cider vinegar

·1 cup water

DIRECTIONS

1.   To prepare the jars, sterilize a minimum of 10-pint jars (or as many as you can). Shuck the corn and remove the silks from the kernels. This is best to perform against a cutting board carefully with a sharp knife.

2.   Transfer the kernels into a large cooking pot, preferably stainless steel. Add all the other ingredients into the pot and stir well, then bring the contents to a boil.

3.   Continue to mix on occasion until the mixture reaches the boiling point, then reduce to medium-low and simmer for about 18 to 20 minutes.

4.   Set the sterilized jars near the stove and gently scoop the corn relish while it's hot with a ladle or large spoon into each jar. Allow for ½ inch at the top of each jar and remove any air bubbles inside.

5. Adjust the level of the relish in each jar and ensure that there is no excess liquid on the rim or edges of the jars. Clean this area thoroughly with a paper towel lightly dampened with vinegar. Affix the lids and close them tightly.

6. Place them in the water bath canner and cover them with at least one inch of water over the jars. Bring the canner to a boil, cover it, and then process for 15 to 16 minutes.

7. Remove from the heat, remove the lid to the canner, and allow the jars of relish to settle for about 5 to 7 minutes before transferring them onto a clean cloth or wire rack.

8. Allow the jars to cool this way, at room temperature, for up to 24 hours. After they have cooled, remove the rings from the lids and wipe the jars well. Place them in a cellar or pantry (away from natural light) for up to one year.

NUTRITION

Calories: 255 Kcal	Carbohydrates: 65 g	Protein: 1.7 g
Fat: 0.3 g	Sugar: 55 g	Cholesterol: 0 mg

165.

CUCUMBER RELISH

 4 Pint Jars   **Prep Time : 60 Mins**   **Cook Time : 60 Mins**

INGREDIENTS

·8 cups chopped cucumbers— stem and blossom ends removed

·1 cup onions, chopped

·2 cups sweet red peppers, chopped

·2 cups sweet green peppers, chopped

·1 tbsp turmeric

·½ cup pickling salt

·8 cups cold water

·2 cups brown sugar, to taste

·4 cups white vinegar

FOR THE SPICE BAG

·1 tbsp mustard seed

·2 medium sticks of cinnamon

·2 tsp whole cloves

·2 tsp whole allspice

DIRECTIONS

1. Rinse and drain vegetables. Remove stems, seeds, and ribs from peppers. Chop and measure all vegetables. Sprinkle with turmeric.

2. Dissolve salt in water. Pour over vegetables. Let stand for 3 hours. Drain.

3. Cover vegetables with more cold water. Let stand for one hour. Drain well. Add spice bag and sugar to vinegar. Heat to boiling. Simmer for about 10 minutes.

4. Remove the spice bag. Pour syrup on top of the vegetables. Let stand overnight. Heat until hot throughout. If too dry, add a bit more vinegar.

5. Allow boiling and stirring to distribute heat. Package the hot relish into sterilized hot jars, allowing ¼ inch of headspace.

6. Wipe the jar's rim, set a warm lid, and tighten. Place in a bath canner with boiling water and process for 10 minutes.

NUTRITION

Calories: 318 Kcal   Carbohydrates: 1 g

Fat: 1 g   Protein: 0 g

BEET RELISH

🥣 **4 Pint Jars** ✂️ **Prep Time : 15 Mins** 🕐 **Cook Time : 20 Mins**

INGREDIENTS

- 1 quart chopped, cooked beets
- 2 quart chopped cabbage
- 1 cup chopped onion
- 1 cup chopped sweet red pepper
- 1-½ cup sugar
- 1 tbsp prepared horseradish
- 1 tbsp pickling salt
- 3 cups white vinegar

DIRECTIONS

1. Combine all the fixings in a large pot. Slowly simmer within 10 minutes. Boil, then quickly pack hot into hot jars, leaving ¼ inch of headspace.

2. Wipe the jar's rim; set a warm lid in place and tighten. Place in a bath canner with boiling water and process for 15 minutes.

NUTRITION

Calories: 34 Kcal	Carbohydrates: 8 g
Fat: 0 g	Protein: 0 g

167.

CHOW-CHOW RELISH

🥣 **4 Pint Jars** **Prep Time : 15 Mins** **Cook Time : 40 Mins**

INGREDIENTS

· 1 medium head cabbage, chopped

· 6 medium onions

· 6 sweet green peppers, remove seeds and ribs

· 6 sweet red peppers, remove seeds and ribs

· 2 quart hard green tomatoes

· ¼ cup pickling salt

· 2 tbsp prepared mustard

· 1-½ quart white vinegar

· 2-½ cups sugar

· 1-½ tsp ground ginger

· 2 tbsp mustard seed

· 1 tbsp celery seed

· 1 tbsp mixed whole pickling spice

DIRECTIONS

1. Chop all vegetables in your meat grinder using a coarse blade. Put with salt, then cover. Let it stand in a cool place overnight. Drain.

2. In a large pot, mix mustard with a small amount of vinegar; add the remaining vinegar, sugar, and spices. Let it boil, then simmer within 30 minutes. Add vegetables. Simmer for about 10 minutes.

3. Package the hot relish into sterilized, hot jars, allowing ¼ inch of headspace. Be sure liquid covers vegetables.

4. Wipe the jar's rim; set a warm lid in place and tighten. Place in a bath canner with boiling water and process for 10 minutes.

NUTRITION

Calories: 15 Kcal   Carbohydrates: 0 g

Fat: 0 g   Protein: 0 g

CORN RELISH

🥣 **4 Pint Jars**   ✕ **Prep Time : 15 Mins**   🕐 **Cook Time : 30 Mins**

INGREDIENTS

- 9 cups fresh sweet corn, cut from ears
- 2 cups chopped onions
- 1 cup chopped green peppers, remove stems, seeds, and ribs
- ½ cup chopped red peppers, remove stems, seeds, and ribs
- 1 cup sugar
- 2 tbsp salt
- 1-½ tbsp celery seed
- 1-½ tbsp mustard seed
- 1 tbsp turmeric
- 3 cups cider vinegar

DIRECTIONS

1. Combine chopped vegetables, sugar, salt, spices, plus vinegar, and let it boil.

2. Simmer within 15 minutes, covered, stirring occasionally to prevent scorching. Ladle hot relish into hot, sterilized jars, leaving ¼ inch of headspace.

3. Wipe the jar's rim; set a warm lid in place and tighten. Place in a bath canner with boiling water and process for 15 minutes.

NUTRITION

Calories: 21 Kcal	Carbohydrates: 4.7 g
Fat: 0.2 g	Protein: 0 g

169.

FRESH CHERRY TOMATO RELISH

🥣 1   **Prep Time : 15 Mins**   **Cook Time : 5 Mins**

INGREDIENTS

·½ cup cherry tomatoes, quartered

·1 splash olive oil

·1 splash red wine vinegar

·1 garlic clove crushed

·Kosher salt, to taste

·Ground black pepper, to taste

DIRECTIONS

1. Mix tomatoes, red wine vinegar, olive oil, salt, garlic, and pepper in a mixing bowl. Cover the bowl with plastic wrap and chill for 30 minutes, or until the flavors have melded and the liquid has accumulated.

2. Return the tomatoes to the bowl after straining the juices into a normal saucepan. Cook the juices over normal heat for 2 to 3 minutes, or until the liquid has reduced and the sauce has a syrupy consistency.

3. Return the sauce to the bowl with the tomatoes and mix.

NUTRITION

Calories: 68 Kcal   Protein: 0.8 g

Carbohydrates: 5.4 g   Fat: 5.3 g

PICKLED PEPPER & ONION RELISH

🥣 **6 Jars**   🍴 **Prep Time : 30 Mins**   🕐 **Cook Time : 40 Mins**

INGREDIENTS

· 3 onions, thin slices
· 8 green bell peppers, thin strips
· 3 jalapeno peppers, minced and seeded
· 6 tbsp pickling spice
· 2 cups white sugar
· 1 tsp salt
· 2 cups apple cider vinegar

DIRECTIONS

1.   In a large saucepan, combine the onion, jalapeño pepper, bell pepper, pickling spice, salt, sugar, and vinegar.

2.   Stir to a boil over high temp, then lower to medium-low heat and cook, stirring periodically, for 5 minutes.

3.   Fill hot, sterilized canning jars halfway with pepper mixture and ¼ inch headspace with hot vinegar.

4.   Top with a sanitized lid and fasten the tops with a screwdriver.

5.   Cover the jars with 2 inches of water in a canner or large stockpot.

6.   Bring to a boil, then lower to low heat and cook for 30 minutes, stirring occasionally.

7.   Remove the jars after 30 minutes and set them aside to cool to room temperature.

8.   These jars that did not seal should be refrigerated.

9.   After opening, keep refrigerated.

NUTRITION

Calories: 17 Kcal	Protein: 0.1 g
Carbohydrates: 4.1 g	Fat: 0.2 g

171.

AUTUMN HARVEST RELISH

 24 | Prep Time : 30 Mins | ⏱ Cook Time : 15 Mins

INGREDIENTS

- 8 cups peeled & chopped apples
- 2½ cups cane sugar
- 2½ cups water
- 1 (12 oz) package of fresh cranberries
- ½ cup red wine vinegar
- 1 cup chopped walnuts
- ¼ cup crystallized ginger
- ¼ tsp ground nutmeg

DIRECTIONS

1. In a large saucepan, combine the sugar, apples, cranberries, water, and vinegar; bring to a boil.

2. Reduce heat to low and cook for 20 minutes until the cranberries begin to break down. Cook until apples are cooked and relish flavors have mingled, 10 to 15 minutes longer after adding walnuts, ginger, and nutmeg to the apple mixture.

3. Fill jars halfway with relish and set aside to cool before covering them with lids. Refrigerate.

NUTRITION

Calories: 91 Kcal   Protein: 0.9 g

Carbohydrates: 15.6 g   Fat: 0.2 g

CRANBERRY ORANGE RELISH

🥣 8   ✕ **Prep Time : 10 Mins**   🕐 **Cook Time : 25 Mins**

INGREDIENTS

- 1 navel orange
- 1 (12 oz) package of fresh cranberries
- ½ cup white sugar
- ⅛ tsp ground cinnamon

DIRECTIONS

1. Take 2 tbsp orange zest and discard the remaining peel and pith. Separate the orange into pieces.

2. In a food processor, pulse orange sections, cranberries, orange zest, sugar, and cinnamon until finely chopped.

3. Place relish in a bowl and cover; chill for at least 2 hours to enable flavors to combine.

NUTRITION

Calories: 76 Kcal   Protein: 0.3 g

Carbohydrates: 19.8 g   Fat: 0.1 g

173.

GREEN TOMATO RELISH

 12 Pints   Prep Time : 75 Mins   Cook Time : 45 Mins

INGREDIENTS

·24 green tomatoes

·3 red bell peppers, seeded and halved

·3 green bell peppers

·12 large onions

·3 tbsp celery seed

·3 tbsp mustard seed

·1 tbsp salt

·5 cups white sugar

·2 cups cider vinegar

DIRECTIONS

1. Coarsely crush tomatoes, green bell peppers, red bell peppers, and onions in a grinder or food processor. (This may have to be done in batches.) Line a big colander with cheesecloth and set it in the sink or a large bowl to drain the tomato mixture for 1 hour.

2. Combine tomato combination, mustard seed, celery seed, sugar, salt, and vinegar in a large non-aluminum stockpot. Bring to a boil, then reduce to low heat and cook for 5 minutes, stirring constantly.

3. Ensure that enough jars and lids are sterilized to contain relish. Fill sterilized jars with relish, ensuring sure there are no gaps or air pockets. Fill jars to the very top. Lids must be screwed on.

4. Fill a big stockpot halfway with the boiling water and place a rack in the bottom. Using a holder, carefully drop the jars into the saucepan. Allow 2 inches between each jar. If required, add additional boiling water until the tops of the jars are covered by 2" of water.

5. Remove jars from the saucepan and lay them several inches apart on a cloth-covered or wood surface to cool. Once cool, squeeze the top of each lid with your finger to ensure a firm seal. Relish may be kept for up to a year in the refrigerator.

NUTRITION

Calories: 32 Kcal	Protein: 0.5 g
Carbohydrates: 7.6 g	Fat: 0.1 g

218

CHAPTER 10: SALSA AND SAUCES

174.

CHOCOLATE SAUCE

🥣 48   ✂️ **Prep Time : 10 Mins**   🕐 **Cook Time : 20 Mins**

INGREDIENTS

- 3 cups sugar
- 1½ cup water
- 1½ cup Dutch-processed cocoa powder
- 2 tbsp light corn syrup
- 1 tbsp vanilla extract
- ¼ tsp salt

DIRECTIONS

1. Add sugar and water over medium heat and cook until boiling in a heavy-bottomed stainless steel saucepan.
2. Add the cocoa powder, corn syrup, vanilla extract, and salt and with a wire whisk, beat until well combined.
3. Cook for about 14 to 15 minutes, stirring frequently.
4. In 3 (1-pint) hot sterilized jars, divide the sauce, leaving about ½-inch space from the top.
5. Slide a small knife around the insides of each jar to remove air bubbles.
6. Wipe any trace of food off the rims of jars with a clean, moist kitchen towel.
7. Close each jar with a lid and screw on the ring.
8. Arrange the jars in a boiling water canner and process for about 15 minutes.
9. Remove the jars from the water canner and place them onto a wooden surface several inches apart to cool completely.
10. After cooling, with your finger press the top of each jar's lid to ensure that the seal is tight.
11. The canned sauce can be stored in the refrigerator for up to 1 month.

NUTRITION

			Fiber: 0.8 g
Calories: 56 Kcal	Total Fat: 0.4 g	Sodium: 13 mg	Sugar: 12.8 g
Cholesterol: 0 mg	Saturated Fat: 0.2 g	Total Carbohydrates: 14.6 g	Protein: 0.5 g

CRAB CAKES

🥣 8   🍴 **Prep Time : 20 Mins**   🕐 **Cook Time : 30 Mins**

INGREDIENTS

- 3 tbsp olive oil
- ½ cup red bell pepper
- cup onion
- ¼ cup celery
- ½ tsp Old Bay seasoning
- 1 lb lump crabmeat
- ½ cup mayonnaise
- 1½ tsp cilantro
- 1 tsp salt
- ½ tsp black pepper
- 2 cups white breadcrumbs
- Eastern Shore Corn Relish
- Lemon wedges

DIRECTIONS

1. Heat 2 tsp (10 ml) olive oil in a medium pan over medium-low heat. Combine the bell pepper and the following 2 ingredients in a mixing bowl. Cook, occasionally stirring, for 8 minutes or until very tender but not brown. Add the Old Bay seasoning and mix well. Remove from the heat and set aside to cool fully.

2. Meanwhile, choose crabmeat and discard any shell fragments. In a large mixing bowl, combine the vegetable combination, mayonnaise, and the next 3 ingredients. Fold in the crabmeat and 12 cups (125 mL) of breadcrumbs gently. Form the ingredients into 8 (12-inch/1-cm) cakes using damp palms. Place the remaining 112 cups (375 mL) of breadcrumbs on a shallow plate. Place cakes on a baking sheet, dredged in breadcrumbs, and softly pressed to adhere. Refrigerate for 30 minutes or until firm.

3. Heat half of the remaining oil in a large skillet over medium-high heat. Cook for 2 to 3 minutes on each side or until golden, adding 4 crab cakes at a time. Using paper towels, absorb any excess liquid. Rep with the remaining oil and the last 4 crab cakes. Serve with lemon wedges and Eastern Shore Corn Relish.

NUTRITION

Calories: 210 Kcal	Fat: 9.88 g
Carbohydrates: 32.18 g	Protein: 9.33 g

CHIPOTLE TOMATILLO SALSA

12   Prep Time : 10 Mins   Cook Time : 15 Mins

INGREDIENTS

- 2 lb tomatillos
- 1 small onion
- 4 garlic cloves
- ¼ cup lime juice
- ½ tsp salt
- 3 to 4 canned chipotle peppers in adobo sauce

DIRECTIONS

1. Preheat the oven to 425°F (220°C). On a large rimmed baking sheet, arrange tomatillos stem side down and onion quarters skin side down. Using a tiny piece of aluminum foil, wrap the garlic cloves. Place a foil bag in one of the baking sheet's corners. Bake for 20 minutes at 425°F (220°C) or until tomatillos and onion begin to brown and soften. To cool, place the baking sheet on a wire rack. Remove skins and throw them in a food processor after the veggies are cold enough to handle.

2. Combine the lime juice and the other ingredients in a food processor and blend until smooth.

3. Fill a big stainless steel or enameled saucepan halfway with the contents. Bring the water to a boil. Remove the pan from the heat. Fill a heated jar halfway with salsa, allowing a 12-inch (1-cm) headspace. Remove air bubbles. Wipe the jar's rim. On the jar, place the lid in the middle. Apply the band and tighten it until it is fingertip-tight. In a boiling-water canner, place the jar.

4. Rep until all of the jars are full. Adjust for altitude and process jars for 25 minutes. Remove jars from heat, remove lids, and set aside for 5 minutes. Remove the jars and set them aside to cool.

NUTRITION

Calories: 205 Kcal	Fat: 9.44 g
Carbohydrates: 31.22 g	Protein: 9.24 g

SMOKY SOUR CHERRY TEQUILA SALSA

4 Jars   Prep Time : 10 Mins   Cook Time : 15 Mins

INGREDIENTS

- 2 cups onion
- ½ cup brown sugar
- ¼ cup lime juice
- 1 garlic clove
- 4 lb cherries
- ½ cup cilantro
- 2 canned chipotle peppers in adobo sauce
- 1 small red serrano pepper
- ¼ cup tequila
- 1½ tsp salt
- ½ tsp black pepper

DIRECTIONS

1. Combine the first 4 ingredients in large stainless steel. Cook for 5 minutes over medium heat, stirring often. Cook for 5 minutes, often stirring, after adding the cherries and the following 3 ingredients. Combine the tequila, salt, and pepper in a mixing bowl. Bring the water to a boil. Remove the pan from the heat.

2. Fill a heated jar halfway with salsa, allowing a 12-inch (1-cm) headspace. Air bubbles should be removed. Wipe the jar's rim. On the jar, place the lid in the middle. Apply the band and tighten it until it is fingertip-tight. In a boiling-water canner, place the jar. Rep until all of the jars are full.

3. Adjust for altitude and process jars for 15 minutes. Remove jars from heat, remove lids, and set aside for 5 minutes. Remove the jars and set them aside to cool.

NUTRITION

Calories: 200 Kcal	Fat: 9.52 g
Carbohydrates: 30.08 g	Protein: 9.36 g

TOMATO SALSA

🥣 **8 Pint Jars**   ✂️ **Prep Time : 30 Mins**   🕐 **Cook Time : 55 Mins**

INGREDIENTS

- 5 lb paste-type Roma tomatoes
- 2 ½ cups chopped onions
- 1 tbsp chopped fresh cilantro, optional
- Plastic or rubber gloves
- 2 cups chopped fresh green chilies
- ¼ cup chopped jalapeño pepper
- ½ tsp garlic powder
- 1 tbsp salt
- ½ tbsp black pepper
- 1 tbsp ground cumin, optional
- 1 ½ tbsp dried oregano, optional
- 1 cup bottled lime juice

DIRECTIONS

1. Boil the tomatoes, then put them aside to cool. Cut the veggies after removing the skins. A total of 14 cups are required. Combine tomatoes, onions, cilantro (if using), chills, and jalapeno in a large saucepan. Bring the mixture to a boil, lower to low heat and constantly whisk for another 10 minutes.

2. After adding the herbs, spices, and lime juice, simmer for 20 minutes. Allow a 12-inch headspace in jars by filling them halfway with salsa. The procedure should be finished when the bubbles have been eliminated, the rims have been cleaned, and the lids have been put in. Wear gloves and keep your hands away from your face while chopping hot peppers. They have the capability of causing severe burns.

Remove the pepper's stem and tip, then cut it in half using a sharp knife. The white membrane that houses the seeds accounts for a considerable percentage of the pepper's "hot." Scrape away the seeds and most of the white membrane with your thumb or a spoon. It's simpler to do this when the water is flowing.

3. Salsa recipes combine acidic tomatoes with nonacidic additives, and the amounts required for safe water-bath canning should not be altered. Measure the items once they've been washed and chopped. Don't assume that a certain quantity of fresh produce will provide the recipe's required amount. When switching to hotter or softer peppers, use care and remember that the total pepper proportion should not be changed. Lime juice may be substituted with lemon juice.

NUTRITION

Calories: 162 Kcal	Carbohydrates: 25.7 g
Fat: 0.86 g	Protein: 5.82 g

CARAMELIZED PINEAPPLE HABANERO SALSA

4 Jars   **Prep Time : 10 Mins**   **Cook Time : 15 Mins**

INGREDIENTS

- 2 ripe pineapples
- Vegetable cooking spray
- 6 tbsp sugar
- 2 cups red onion
- ½ cup lime juice
- 1 habanero pepper
- ½ cup fresh cilantro
- 1½ tsp salt

DIRECTIONS

1. Preheat the oven to 400°F/200°C. Each pineapple quarter should be cut into 1-inch slices crosswise. Place slices on 2 baking pans that have been sprayed with cooking spray in a single layer. 14 cups (60 mL) sugar, equally distributed.

2. Preheat the oven to 400°F/200°C and bake for 15 minutes. Turn the slices over and bake for another 10 to 15 minutes, or until they start to caramelize. Remove from the oven and set aside to cool. 6 to 12 cups pineapple slices, coarsely chopped (1.6 L). In a large stainless steel or enameled saucepan, combine the pineapple, onion, and the following 2 ingredients. Over medium heat, bring to a boil. Cook for 5 minutes, stirring once in a while. Combine cilantro, salt, and the remaining 2 tbsp (30 mL) sugar in a mixing bowl.

3. Place half of the pineapple mixture in a food processor and pulse until finely chopped. (Avoid pureeing.) Return the chopped mixture to the remaining roughly chopped pineapple mixture in the pan. Cook, stirring periodically, for 5 minutes over medium heat, or until well cooked.

4. Fill a heated jar halfway with salsa, allowing a 12-inch (1-cm) headspace. Remove air bubbles. Wipe the jar's rim. On the jar, place the lid in the middle. Apply the band and tighten it until it is fingertip-tight. In a boiling-water canner, place the jar. Rep until all of the jars are full. Adjust for altitude and process jars for 15 minutes. Remove jars from heat, remove lids, and set aside for 5 minutes. Remove the jars and set them aside to cool.

NUTRITION

Calories: 168 Kcal	Carbohydrates: 28.7 g
Fat: 0.46 g	Protein: 2.82 g

180.

SALSA ROJA

 3 Jars 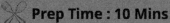 **Prep Time : 10 Mins** **Cook Time : 15 Mins**

INGREDIENTS

- 1¼ lb plum tomatoes
- 1 small onion
- 6 garlic cloves
- 6 ancho chills
- 2 cups of water
- ¼ cup fresh lime juice
- Salt to taste
- Black pepper to taste

DIRECTIONS

1.   Preheat the oven to 400°F/200°C. Place the tomatoes and onion quarters on a wide-rimmed baking sheet, skin side down. Wrap a tiny piece of aluminum foil around the garlic cloves. Place a foil bag in one of the baking sheet's corners.

2.   Bake for 20 minutes at 425°F (220°C) or until tomatoes and onion begin to brown and soften. To cool, place the baking sheet on a wire rack. While the veggies are roasting, toast the ancho chills for 8 to 9 seconds on each side on a hot grill or in a pan, or until they puff and blister. (Don't let them burn, or they'll become bitter.)

Remove stems and seeds when chills are cool enough to handle; rip them into big pieces and put them in a medium basin. Fill the pot halfway with boiling water. Allow for 15 minutes of softening time. Drain and save the soaking liquid.

3. Remove the skins from the roasted veggies when they are cold enough to handle, and set them in a food processor. Add the lime juice, and ancho chills, and puree until smooth, adding a little of the leftover soaking liquid to get the desired consistency. Season to taste with salt and pepper. In a large stainless steel or enameled saucepan, transfer the salsa. Bring the water to a boil. Remove the pan from the heat.

4. Fill a heated jar halfway with salsa, allowing a 12-inch (1-cm) headspace. Air bubbles should be removed. Wipe the jar's rim. On the jar, place the lid in the middle. Apply the band and tighten it until it is fingertip-tight. In a boiling-water canner, place the jar. Rep until all of the jars are full. Adjust for altitude and process jars for 25 minutes. Remove jars from heat, remove lids, and set aside for 5 minutes. Remove the jars and set them aside to cool.

NUTRITION

Calories: 142 Kcal	Carbohydrates: 24.7 g
Fat: 0.46 g	Protein: 5.12 g

ROASTED SALSA VERDE

🥣 3 Jars | ✕ Prep Time : 10 Mins | 🕐 Cook Time : 15 Mins

INGREDIENTS

- ·4 lb tomatillos
- ·2 medium-sized white onions
- ·2 jalapeño or serrano peppers
- ·6 garlic cloves
- ·½ cup lime juice
- ·¼ cup cilantro leaves
- ·2 tsp salt
- ·1 tsp black pepper

DIRECTIONS

1. Preheat the oven to 425°F (220°C). Arrange tomatillos on a large rimmed baking sheet coated with aluminum foil, stem side down. Place the onions, jalapeno peppers, and garlic on the baking sheet that has been prepped. Bake for 15 minutes at 425°F (220°C) or until the garlic is softened. Remove the garlic cloves from the baking sheet. Bake for another 15 minutes, or until the onion is soft and the tomatillos and peppers have browned somewhat. Remove from the oven and set aside to cool somewhat. Remove the stems and seeds when the peppers are cool enough to handle.

2. Blend roasted veggies and garlic in batches until smooth in a food processor. Transfer to stainless steel or enameled 4-quart (4-L) saucepan. Combine the lime juice and the other ingredients in a mixing bowl. Bring to a low boil, then reduce to low heat. Remove the pan from the heat. Fill a heated jar halfway with salsa, allowing a 12-inch (1-cm) headspace.

3. Air bubbles should be removed. Wipe the jar's rim. On the jar, place the lid in the middle. Apply the band and tighten it until it is fingertip-tight. In a boiling-water canner, place the jar. Rep until all of the jars are full. Adjust for altitude and process the jars for 20 minutes. Remove jars from heat, remove lids, and set aside for 5 minutes. Remove the jars and set them aside to cool.

NUTRITION

Calories: 155 Kcal

Fat: 0.66 g

Carbohydrates: 20.7 g

Protein: 5.82 g

182.

CORN AND AVOCADO SALSA

🥣 **10 Pints** ✂️ **Prep Time : 30 Mins** 🕐 **Cook Time : 0 Mins**

INGREDIENTS

- 4 avocados, diced
- 2 cups frozen corn kernels, thawed
- 1 small onion, chopped
- 1 red bell pepper, chopped
- ½ cup sliced ripe olives, drained
- 1 tsp dried oregano
- 5 garlic cloves, minced
- 3 tbsp cider vinegar
- ¼ cup lemon juice
- cup olive oil
- ½ tsp salt
- ½ tsp pepper

DIRECTIONS

1. In a bowl, combine onion, red bell pepper, olives, and corn.

2. In a small bowl, set together apple cider vinegar, lemon juice, olive oil, oregano, garlic, salt, and pepper until well merged; pour into the corn mixture and toss until well coated. Transfer to sterile jars or cans and seal. Refrigerate until ready to serve.

NUTRITION

Calories: 81 Kcal	Total Carbohydrates: 6.1 g
Total Fat: 6.5 g	Protein: 1.1 g

FRESH GREEN SALSA

12 Pint Jars **Prep Time : 10 Mins** **Cook Time : 30 Mins**

INGREDIENTS

- 2 jalapeno peppers, diced
- 6 green onions, sliced
- 7 cups tomatoes, diced
- 4 garlic cloves, minced
- 2 tbsp minced cilantro
- 4 drops of hot pepper sauce
- 2 tbsp lime juice
- ½ cup vinegar
- 2 tsp salt

DIRECTIONS

1. Merge all ingredients in a pan, set to a boil, and then simmer for 15 minutes. Ladle in sterile jars and seal.

2. Bring a hot water bath for about 15 minutes and then let cool before storing in the fridge.

NUTRITION

Calories: 5 Kcal	Total Carbohydrates: 0.4 g
Total Fat: 0 g	Protein: 0.2 g

MILD JALAPEÑO TOMATO SALSA

🥣 10 Pints ✖️ Prep Time : 40 Mins 🕐 Cook Time : 30 Mins

INGREDIENTS

- 10 ½ lb tomatoes, peeled, quartered
- 3 large onions, chopped
- 4 medium green peppers, chopped
- 1 medium sweet red pepper, chopped
- 1 celery rib, chopped
- 4 jalapeño peppers, seeded, chopped
- 24 oz tomato paste
- ¼ tsp hot pepper sauce
- 1 ¾ cup white vinegar
- ½ cup sugar
- 15 garlic cloves, minced
- ¼ cup canning salt

DIRECTIONS

1. In a large stockpot, cook tomatoes over medium heat, for 20 minutes, uncovered. Drain, reserving 2 cups liquid. Return tomatoes to the pot.

2. Add the remaining ingredients and the reserved tomato liquid. Bring to a boil. Reduce heat and let simmer for 1 hour, frequently stirring, uncovered.

3. Scoop the hot mixture into hot sterilized 1-pint jars, leaving ¼-inch space on the top. Screw on bands until fingertip tight. Place caps on jars and screw on bands until fingertip tight.

4. Set jars into a canner, ensuring that they are completely covered with water. Let boil for 20 minutes. Remove jars and cool.

NUTRITION

Calories: 14 Kcal	Total Carbohydrates: 3 g
Total Fat: 0 g	Protein: 0 g

ROASTED TOMATO CHIPOTLE SAUCE

4 Jars | **Prep Time : 60 Mins** | **Cook Time : 20 Mins**

INGREDIENTS

·1½ oz cascabel chilies, seeded & roasted

·2 oz chipotle chilies, seeded & roasted

·3 lb Italian plum tomatoes, peeled, roasted, & chopped

·½ lb small onions, peeled, roasted, & chopped

·1 lb green peppers, peeled roasted, & chopped

·1 head garlic, peeled, roasted, & chopped

·2 tsp granulated sugar

·1cup vinegar

·1 tsp salt

DIRECTIONS

1. Place roasted chilies in a medium container with 2 cups of boiling water. To drown the chilies, place a weight on top of them. Allow it to soak for a while.

2. In a large saucepot, combine the tomatoes, onions, garlic cloves, & peppers and cook over medium heat. Purée the chilies with soaking water and add to the roasted vegetables, along with the vinegar, salt, & sugar. Allow it to come to a boil, stirring often, and then continue to simmer for another 15 minutes. Remove the pan from the heat and set it aside to cool.

3. Fill each canning jar halfway with spicy sauce. Keep in mind that one inch of headroom is required. Remove air bubbles with a spatula, then wash jar rims with a clean cloth, adjust the lids, and turn the screw band on.

4. Place the filled jars in a pressure canner with a dial-gauge pressure of 11 lb or a weighted-gauge pressure of 10 lb. Heat the jars in the oven for 20 minutes, adjusting for the altitude. Turn off the heat and let the pressure naturally decrease. Remove the lids & let the jars cool for 5 minutes in the canner. Remove the jars and set them aside to cool. After 24 hours, check the seals on the lids.

NUTRITION

Calories: 272 Kcal	Protein: 35.8g
Carbohydrates: 0.8 g	Fat: 14 g

186.

TOMATO AND JALAPEÑO SAUCE

 5 Jars   **Prep Time : 15 Mins**   **Cook Time : 60 Mins**

INGREDIENTS

- ·2 cups sliced onions
- ·7 cups seeded & sliced tomatoes
- ·8 jalapeño peppers, seeded & chopped
- ·1 cup green bell pepper
- ·1 can tomato paste
- ·3 garlic cloves, crushed
- ·½ cup packed chopped cilantro
- ·½ tsp ground cumin
- ·¾ cup white vinegar

DIRECTIONS

1. Combine onions, tomatoes, green pepper, jalapeño pepper, tomato paste, cilantro, cumin, garlic, and vinegar in a large saucepot. Bring to a boil over medium-high heat. Reduce heat to low and occasionally stir for approximately 30 minutes, or until salsa reaches desired consistency.

2. Fill each canning jar halfway with sauce. Keep a one-inch headspace in mind. Remove air bubbles with the spatula, then wash jar rims with a clean cloth, adjust the lids, and the screw band on.

3. Place the filled jars in a pressure canner with a dial-gauge pressure of 11 lb or a weighted-gauge pressure of 10 lb. Heat the jars in the oven for 20 minutes, adjusting for altitude. Turn off the heat and let the pressure naturally decrease. Remove the lids and let the jars cool for 5 minutes in the canner. Remove the jars and set them aside to cool. After 24 hours, check the seals on the lids.

4. Serve with hot dogs, roast beef, cold roast chicken, and spring rolls, as well as other Western and Asian meals.

NUTRITION

Calories: 269 Kcal	Protein: 15 g
Carbohydrates: 45 g	Fat: 4 g

FIESTA TOMATOES SAUCE

8 Jars **Prep Time : 15 Mins** **Cook Time : 75 Mins**

INGREDIENTS

- 18 cups thinly chopped tomatoes
- ¾ cup vinegar
- 189 g (1 can) fiesta salsa mix

DIRECTIONS

1. Combine tomatoes, and vinegar in a big saucepot over medium-high heat. Allow mixture to boil, stirring often. Reduce the heat to low and cook for 5 minutes.

2. Into each canning jar, ladle the heated salsa. Keep a one-inch headspace in mind. Remove air bubbles with the spatula, then wash jar rims with a clean cloth, adjust the lids, and the screw band on.

3. Place the filled jars in a pressure canner with a dial-gauge pressure of 11 lb or a weighted-gauge pressure of 10 lb. Heat the jars in the oven for 75 minutes, adjusting for the altitude. Turn off the heat and let the pressure naturally decrease.

4. Remove the lids and let the jars cool for 5 minutes in the canner. Remove the jars and set them aside to cool. After 24 hours, check the seals on the lids.

NUTRITION

Calories: 272 Kcal
Carbohydrates: 0.8 g

Protein: 35.8 g
Fat: 14 g

UNRIPE TOMATO SALSA

 8 Pints   Prep Time : 30 Mins Cook Time : 60 Mins

INGREDIENTS

- 5 lb unpeeled green tomatoes, chopped
- 6 yellow onions, chopped small
- 3 jalapeños, chopped with the seeds
- 4 large green bell peppers, chopped
- 6 garlic cloves, minced
- 1 cup fresh cilantro, chopped
- 1 cup lime juice
- 1 tbsp salt
- ½ tbsp cumin
- 1 tbsp dried oregano leaves
- 2 tbsp pepper

DIRECTIONS

1. Combine the ingredients in a large pot, then bring to a boil, mixing for the next 30 to 40 minutes.

2. After the time is up and at a boil again, put the salsa into the sterilized jars. Allow 15 minutes for the jars to soak in the water bath.

3. Let sit at room temperature for about 24 hours before refrigerating or storing.

NUTRITION

Calories: 67 Kcal	Total Carbohydrates: 17 g
Total Fat: 0 g	Protein: 0 g

CRANBERRY SAUCE

🥣 **4 Pints**   ✗ **Prep Time : 15 Mins**   **Cook Time : 55 Mins**

INGREDIENTS

·4 cups sugar, granulated
·4 x 12-oz bags of
cranberries, fresh
·1 fresh orange, juiced, +
add water to make 4 cups
liquid total
·1 orange zest

DIRECTIONS

1. Combine water, zest, orange juice, and sugar in a large stockpot on high heat. Bring to a boil.
2. Add cranberries. Return to boil. Lower heat. Boil gently for about 10 minutes. Cranberries will pop open.
3. Pour into a sieve over a heat-safe bowl until all left is a paste with twigs and seeds from orange zest and cranberries.
4. Pour into hot, sterile canning jars. Leave ¼" of headspace. Wipe rims and place lids on jars. Screw on until fingertip tight.
5. Place jars in canner. Cover using hot water. Bring to a boil. Process for 15 minutes. Turn the heat off.
6. Remove the cover from the canner. Leave jars inside for about 5 minutes and transfer to a towel or rack to cool, undisturbed, overnight.
7. Wipe jars down and label them. Store in a cool, dark place for as long as 12 months.

NUTRITION

Calories: 110 Kcal   Fat: 0 g
Carbohydrates: 25 g   Protein: 0 g

FRESH SUMMER TOMATO SAUCE

🥣 **8 Pints** ✕ **Prep Time : 15 Mins** 🕐 **Cook Time : 30 Mins**

INGREDIENTS

- ·2 tbsp extra-virgin olive oil
- ·3 garlic cloves, minced
- ·1 red onion, chopped
- ·3 lb tomatoes, halved
- ·A pinch of red pepper flakes
- ·½ tsp chopped thyme
- ·1 tsp chopped oregano
- ·1 tsp chopped basil
- ·1 tbsp chopped parsley
- ·A pinch of sea salt
- ·A pinch of pepper

DIRECTIONS

1. Preheat a nonstick skillet over medium heat; add in oil and sauté onion and garlic for about 3 minutes or until fragrant.

2. Stir in tomatoes, red pepper flakes, thyme, oregano, basil, parsley, salt, and black pepper, and lower the heat. Cover and simmer for about 30 minutes.

3. Remove the pan from the heat and purée the sauce until smooth in a food processor. Fill sterilized jars halfway with the mixture and close them tightly.

4. Allow cooling before freezing after processing in a hot water bath for about 5 minutes.

NUTRITION

Calories: 70 Kcal   Fat: 4 g

Carbohydrates: 6 g   Protein: 3 g

HOMEMADE PIZZA SAUCE

🥣 4 Pints   ✂ Prep Time : 15 Mins   🕐 Cook Time : 80 Mins

INGREDIENTS

- 2 tbsp chopped parsley
- 28 ripe tomatoes
- 1 tsp celery seed
- 2 yellow onions
- 3 tbsp olive oil
- 1 tsp black pepper
- 1 tbsp oregano
- 1 tbsp dry basil
- 2 tbsp lemon juice
- 1 tsp dry rosemary
- 4 garlic cloves
- 2 tsp kosher salt
- 1 tbsp white sugar

DIRECTIONS

1. Peel the tomatoes. Blanch for 2 to 3 minutes in boiling water so that they are easier to peel. Puree them in a blender or food processor. Mince the onions and garlic cloves.

2. Sauté the onions and garlic in a large saucepan with olive oil for about 3 to 4 minutes until tender and fragrant.

3. Add the tomato puree. Bring to a boil on medium-high heat. Reduce the heat to low and let simmer for 45 minutes. Once the sauce thickens, put it into jars.

4. Boil the jars for approximately 25 minutes in a water bath. Let cool completely before storing.

5. Enjoy on pizza.

NUTRITION

Calories: 40 Kcal   Fat: 3 g

Carbohydrates: 3 g   Protein: 1g

HOMEMADE SPAGHETTI SWEET SAUCE

8 Pints | Prep Time : 15 Mins | Cook Time : 4 Hours

INGREDIENTS

- 4 large onions, cut into wedges
- 4 large green peppers
- 25 lb tomatoes
- ¼ cup canola oil
- 3 cups tomato paste
- 2 tsp dried basil
- 8 garlic cloves, minced
- 2 tsp dried parsley flakes
- 4 tsp dried oregano
- 2 tsp Worcestershire sauce
- ¼ cup salt
- cup sugar
- 2 bay leaves
- 1 cup fresh lemon juice
- 2 tsp red pepper flakes

DIRECTIONS

1. Boil water, add in tomatoes, let boil for about 1 minute, and then plunge them into iced water. Peel off the skin and add to a stockpot.

2. In a food processor, pulse together onions and green peppers until chopped and add to the stockpot. Stir in the remaining ingredients, except lemon juice, and add in water.

3. Cook for about 4 hours and discard the laid leaves. Stir in fresh lemon juice and divide among sterile jars.

4. Seal and process in a hot water bath for about 30 minutes. Remove, let cool and then store in the fridge.

NUTRITION

Calories: 54 Kcal   Fat: 1 g

Carbohydrates: 12 g   Protein: 3 g

HOMEMADE TOMATO SAUCE

4 Jars   **Prep Time : 15 Mins**   **Cook Time : 50 Mins**

INGREDIENTS

- 8 lb ripe tomatoes
- 1 tsp sea salt
- 4 tbsp bottled or jarred lemon juice

DIRECTIONS

1. Rinse and clean the tomatoes. Remove their seeds and skins. Put the peeled or pureed tomatoes into a pot with the salt and then bring it to a boil.

2. Put 1 tbsp lemon juice in each jar and then transfer the tomato sauce into them. Boil the jars for at least 45 minutes.

3. After 45 minutes, remove the jars from the boiling water and let them cool. Store in a cool, dark place afterward.

NUTRITION

Calories: 86 Kcal	Fat: 2 g
Carbohydrates: 16 g	Protein: 4 g

194.

LEMON STRAWBERRY SAUCE

 2 Pints   **Prep Time : 15 Mins**   🕐 **Cook Time : 15 Mins**

INGREDIENTS

- ¼ cup lemon juice
- 2 lb strawberries
- 4 cups granulated sugar

DIRECTIONS

1. In a sizable bowl, use a potato masher to crush the strawberries in batches until you have 3 cups of mashed berries. Leave strawberries intact if you prefer more chunkiness.

2. In a heavy-bottomed, nonreactive pot, mix the strawberries, sugar, and lemon juice. Stir over low heat until the sugar is dissolved, then increase the heat to high and boil for 15 minutes as you stir occasionally.

3. Spoon the sauce into a prepared jar. Use a funnel to transfer the sauce, leaving some headspace safely.

4. Rinse the rims of the jars with a dampened, clean, lint-free cloth or paper towel and once again with a dry towel to remove any sauce or liquid from the rim of the jar.

5. Arrange the canning lid on the jar and twist the canning ring on until it's just snug on the jar.

6. Carefully transfer the jars into the water bath using the canning tongs and place the lid on the canning pot. Start the timer and process in the water bath for 10 minutes.

NUTRITION

Calories: 5 Kcal	Fat: 0 g
Carbohydrates: 1 g	Protein: 0 g

POMEGRANATE BBQ AND STIR FRY SAUCE

🥣 **4 Jars**　　✄ **Prep Time : 10 Mins**　　🕐 **Cook Time : 15 Mins**

INGREDIENTS

- 3 cups chicken stock
- 1½ cup ketchup
- ½ cup brown sugar
- ½ cup soy sauce
- ½ cup pomegranate molasses
- 1 tbsp Worcester shire Sauce
- 2 tsp coarsely chopped fresh ginger
- 2 garlic cloves
- 2 small serrano chills
- 1 cinnamon stick
- ½ star anise
- ½ cup granulated sugar

DIRECTIONS

1.　In a large stainless steel, combine the first 11 ingredients. Bring to a boil over medium heat; decrease the heat to low and cook for 20 minutes, uncovered. Pour the mixture into a basin through a wire-mesh strainer, discarding the particles. Put the sauce back in the pan. Bring to a boil, whisking continually until the sugar has dissolved. Remove the pan from the heat.

2.　Fill a heated jar with hot sauce, leaving a 14-inch (5-cm) headspace. Air bubbles should be removed. Wipe the jar's rim. On the jar, place the lid in the middle. Apply the band and tighten it until it is fingertip-tight. In a boiling-water canner, place the jar. Rep until all of the jars are full.

3.　Adjust for altitude and process jars for 10 minutes. Remove jars from heat, remove lids, and set aside for 5 minutes. Remove the jars and set them aside to cool.

NUTRITION

Calories: 154 Kcal	Fat: 1.08 g
Carbohydrates: 51.2 g	Protein: 4.87 g

196.

CHERRY BOURBON BBQ SAUCE

🥣 3 Jars | ✂️ Prep Time : 10 Mins | 🕐 Cook Time : 15 Mins

INGREDIENTS

- ·1 cup cherries
- · cup bourbon
- ·1 cup onion
- ·1 tbsp olive oil
- ·1 tsp smoked paprika
- ·1 garlic clove
- ·½ cup apple cider vinegar
- ·½ cup dark brown sugar
- ·1½ cup tomato sauce
- ·1 tbsp dry mustard
- ·1 tbsp Worcestershire sauce
- ·1 tsp salt
- ·¼ tsp black pepper
- ·1 tsp prepared horseradish,

DIRECTIONS

1. In a microwave-safe bowl, combine cherries and bourbon. Microwave on HIGH for 30 seconds, covered. Remove from the equation. In medium stainless steel, sauté onion in heated olive oil for 5 to 7 minutes or until the onion is soft. Cook, stirring regularly, for 1 minute, until paprika and garlic are fragrant. Cook for 2 to 3 minutes, or until syrupy, after adding the vinegar and brown sugar.

2. If using, stir in the tomato sauce, the following 4 ingredients, and the horseradish. Bring to a low boil, then reduce to low heat and cook for 20 minutes, stirring periodically. Stir in the reserved cherry mixture and cook, uncovered, for 5 minutes, stirring often. Remove from the heat and let it cool slightly.

3. In a blender, puree the sauce until it is smooth. Bring back to a boil in the saucepan. Fill a heated jar with hot sauce, leaving a 14-inch (5-cm) headspace. Air bubbles should be removed. Wipe the jar's rim. On the jar, place the lid in the middle. Apply the band and tighten it until it is fingertip-tight. In a boiling-water canner, place the jar. Rep until all of the jars are full. Adjust for altitude and process jars for 15 minutes. Remove jars from heat, remove lids, and set aside for 5 minutes. Remove the jars and set them aside to cool.

NUTRITION

Calories: 344 Kcal	Fat: 1.08 g
Carbohydrates: 81.06 g	Protein: 6.07 g

SPICY ASIAN PLUM SAUCE

🥣 4 Jars   🍴 Prep Time : 10 Mins   🕐 Cook Time : 15 Mins

INGREDIENTS

- 4 lb black or red plums
- 1½ cup light brown sugar
- ½ cup rice vinegar or apple cider vinegar
- ¼ cup lite soy sauce
- 1 tsp ginger
- 1 medium onion
- 3 garlic cloves
- 1 tsp salt
- 1 tsp red pepper
- ½ tsp fennel seeds
- ½ tsp Szechuan peppercorns or black peppercorns
- ½ tsp cinnamon
- ½ tsp ginger
- ½ tsp red pepper
- ⅛ tsp cloves
- 2 star anise

DIRECTIONS

1. In a 4-qt. (4-L) stainless steel or enameled Dutch oven, bring the first 7 ingredients to a boil over medium heat; decrease heat and simmer, often stirring, for 20 minutes or until plums and onion are very soft. Combine the salt and the other ingredients in a mixing bowl. Cook, uncovered, for 20 minutes, or until the plums have disintegrated and the mixture has thickened. Remove the star anise and throw it away.

2. In a food processor, puree the plum mixture in batches. Fill a bowl with each batch of purée. Fill a Dutch oven halfway with purée. Over medium heat, bring to a simmer. Remove the pan from the heat. Fill a heated jar with hot sauce, leaving a 14-inch (5-cm) headspace. Air bubbles should be removed. Wipe the jar's rim. On the jar, place the lid in the middle. Apply the band and tighten it until it is fingertip-tight. In a boiling-water canner, place the jar.

3. Rep until all of the jars are full. Adjust for altitude and process jars for 10 minutes. Remove jars from heat, remove lids, and set aside for 5 minutes. Remove the jars and set them aside to cool.

NUTRITION

Calories: 274	Fat: 0.98 g
Carbohydrates: 61.25 g	Protein: 4.87 g

198.

CACCIATORE SIMMER SAUCE

 4 Jars   **Prep Time : 10 Mins**   **Cook Time : 15 Mins**

INGREDIENTS

- 12 lb tomatoes
- 1½ cup onion
- 1 red bell pepper
- 1 cup portobello mushrooms
- ½ cup dry red or dry white wine
- 2 tsp salt
- 1 tsp dried thyme
- 1 tsp dried oregano
- ½ tsp black pepper
- ½ tsp red pepper, optional
- 3 garlic cloves
- 1 bay leaf
- 1 tsp citric acid

DIRECTIONS

1. Preheat the oven to 375°F (190°C). Tomatoes should be washed and dried with paper towels. To produce uniform-sized pieces, cut tomatoes in half or quarters. Arrange the pieces on large baking sheets in a single layer. Bake for 45 minutes at 375°F (190°C) or until very soft and starts to color. Cool.

2. On a large baking sheet, arrange the onion, red bell pepper, and mushrooms in a single layer. Preheat the oven to 375°F (190°C) and bake for 20 minutes, or until golden brown. Fill a 6-qt. (6–L) stainless steel or enameled Dutch oven halfway with the onion mixture. The skins and seeds may be removed by pressing tomatoes through a food mill into a Dutch oven. Skins and seeds should be discarded.

3. Combine the wine and the following 7 ingredients in a mixing bowl. Bring to a boil, lower to low heat and cook uncovered for 20 minutes. Add the citric acid and mix well. Remove the bay leaf and toss it out. Fill a heated jar halfway with hot sauce, allowing a 12-inch (1–cm) headspace. Air bubbles should be removed. Wipe the jar's rim. On the jar, place the lid in the middle. Apply the band and tighten it until it is fingertip-tight. In a boiling-water canner, place the jar. Rep until all of the jars are full. Adjust for altitude and process the jars for 40 minutes. Remove jars from heat, remove lids, and set aside for 5 minutes. Remove the jars and set them aside to cool.

NUTRITION

Calories: 324 Kcal	Fat: 1.66 g
Carbohydrates: 41.26 g	Protein: 3.87 g

CONCLUSION

Thank you for reading this book. Using Amish canning to preserve food ensures that it remains fresh all year round efficiently and cost-effectively. Numerous organizations have made it their sole mission to teach people how to preserve food in small batches to spread the knowledge of home canning. Food preservation is required to maintain the highest possible quality. Amish Canning is a rewarding hobby that also serves as a practical way to store food in your pantry. You are not only being environmentally conscious, but you are also avoiding manufactured foods that have been preserved using unnatural methods to begin with. Use the recipes to get started on your canning adventure. Food conservation has always been a top priority for our people.

Food canning is a deeply satisfying activity. When you look at your canned foods and realize you did it on your own, it will give you the motivation you need to make this a regular habit. If you regularly can your food, you will notice a decrease in the amount of money you spend on produce and other canned foods. Home canning will also have a positive impact on your eating habits. The foods that you will preserve will be far healthier than those found in supermarkets.

You will be unstoppable once you have mastered the art of canning your food! I won't lie to you and tell you that everything will be simple; especially the first few times. You will make a few mistakes, and you may also make a mess of your kitchen. This is to be expected; you are, after all, a beginner. There are numerous reasons why food should be canned. It increases the shelf life of items preserved in this manner while also ensuring that they are not exposed to contaminants in the environment, such as molds or other chemicals.

Canning is a time-consuming and labor-intensive process. Most people who do it all year can enjoy it, but others may only be able to do it in short bursts every now and then. If this describes you or if you're just getting started, we've got some advice for you! Canning your own food is an enjoyable hobby. When you look at your canned foods and realize you did it on your own, you'll have the motivation you need to make this a regular habit. Assume you regularly can food. You will notice a reduction in your spending on produce and other canned foods. Your eating habits will benefit from home canning as well. You will be unstoppable once you have mastered the art of canning your food. You will make a few mistakes and possibly ruin your kitchen. This is to be expected; after all, you are a beginner.

However, as time goes on, the number of mistakes you make will decrease, and you will no longer need the help of this guide. You will be able to develop your own recipes! This has to start with the first steps, which include reading this book. Just keep the reminders in mind, especially the fact that you must first understand the method you intend to use before you begin doing anything.

Thank you very much, and best wishes!

35912182R00137

MW00891438

An Emerald Sea For You + Me, copyright 2020

This work is inspired by my appreciation and love for the sea, and the Scuba diving that brought me to the magic to be found in our underwater world.

My hope is that our young people will also be inspired to appreciate and protect the seas and oceans, this priceless part of our world, which covers approximately 71 percent of it!

ISBN – 979-8-6211471-6-7

This is a work of fiction. Any and all characters and content are products of the author's imagination.

Editing by Philippa Brown

Front cover art and all illustrations by Don Ravensbergen

Written and conceived by author, Don Ravensbergen

Self-published by Don Ravensbergen
British Columbia, Canada
First printing edition 2019 (Sea of Green)
Mailing address
Box 723, Station A, Nanaimo, BC, Canada V9R 5M2
Email
don.ravensbergen@gmail.com
Website
www.vancouver-island-dive-sites.com

Sea of Green

a watery tale...

Splishity splashity sploshity you

Splashity sploshity splishity me

So many creatures beneath the sea

Come float, come swim, come all, and see

What shall we see when see you say

Beneath the waves where eyes can't see

Deep down below away and deep

Where creatures crawl and also creep

Come show yourselves for ponder we do

We long to wiggle and waggle like you

Beneath the waves where eyes can't see

Diver Don said it's amazing to be

With AL – U - minium tanks of air

Some day, some how, we'll visit there

So down down down, away and deep

where fishes swim even while they sleep

So away down deep and far below

Well swim we did and crawl and so

Creatures strange our eyes did see

We saw them and they saw we

Slippery fish and flippery dish

Sights we saw only one could wish

Away down deep under the sea

With Diver Don just him and thee

Crawl and swim we did ourselves

Both high and low among the shells

Some creatures shy and some so meek

Others bold and sassy...full of cheek

We swam with care and gentle ease

Looked not touched and never teased

Below the waves deep and away

floating with currents did we all play

Amazing sea life we did ponder

While here and there did we all wander

The undersea world well it's all theirs

Ours to only visit and sometimes share

So down down down below the waves

Live fish and crabs in rocks and caves

While their young need lots of help

As they learn and grow in beds of kelp

A wonderful world we found below

There is much to see in natures show

As with the tides both lows and highs

The questions flow of whats and whys

Such interesting life both large or small

All shapes and colours come they all

so many sea creatures hidden from above

Ours to respect...care for...and love...

The End

An Emerald Sea For You +Me

Splishity splashity sploshity you
Splashity sploshity splishity me
So many creatures beneath the sea
Come float come swim come all and see

What shall we see when see you say
Beneath the waves where eyes can't see
Deep down below away and deep
Where creatures crawl and also creep

Come show yourselves for ponder we do
We long to wiggle and waggle like you
Beneath the waves where eyes can't see
Diver Don say's it's amazing to be

With AL - U – MINIUM tanks of air
Some day some how we'll visit there
So down down down away and deep
Where fishes swim...while they sleep

So away down deep and far below
Well swim we did and crawl and so...
Creatures strange our eyes did see
We saw them and they saw we

Slippery fish and flippery dish
Sights we saw only one could wish
Away down deep under the sea
With Diver Don just him and thee

Crawl and swim we did ourselves
Both high and low among the shells
Some creatures shy some so meek
Others bold and sassy full of cheek

We swam with care and gentle ease
Looked not touched and never teased
Below the waves deep and away
Floating with currents did we all play

Amazing sea life we did ponder
While here and there did we all wander
The undersea world well its all theirs
Ours only to visit and sometimes share

So down down down below the waves
Live fish and crabs in rocks and caves
While their young need lots of help
As they learn and grow in beds of kelp

A wonderful world we found below
Theres much to see in natures show
As with the tides both lows and highs
The questions flow of whats and whys?

Such interesting life whether large or small
All shapes and sizes come they all
The many undersea creatures hidden from above
Ours to respect...care for...and love...

The End

Made in the USA
Monee, IL
02 February 2021